The 31 Day Pursuit
CHALLENGE

D0464515

WIFE IN PURSUIT

31 DAILY CHALLENGES

FOR LOVING YOUR HUSBAND WELL

By Selena Frederick

CORMENS PRESS

TACOMA, WASHINGTON

WIFE IN PURSUIT

31 Daily Challenges for Loving Your Husband Well

Copyright © 2017 by Ryan and Selena Frederick

Published by Cormens Press
a division of Vilicus Holdings

First Edition

Unless otherwise noted, Scripture quotations are taken from
THE ENGLISH STANDARD VERSION. © 2001 by Crossway
Bibles, a division of Good News Publishers.

Author portrait by Jeff Marsh. Used with permission.

ISBN-10: 0-9974713-3-6

ISBN-13: 978-0-9974713-3-5

(pbk. bw.)

1 3 5 7 9 10 8 6 4 2   21 20 19 18 17

Printed in the United States of America

This book is dedicated to my sweet friend Kerrie.

*You're a constant reminder of God's selfless,
loving pursuit of our hearts.*

I am forever grateful for your friendship.

Contents

A Letter from the Author

A perfect [woman] would never act from a sense of duty; [she'd]
always want the right thing more than the wrong one. Duty
is only a substitute for love (of God and of other people) like a
crutch which is a substitute for a leg. Most of us need the crutch
at times; but of course it is idiotic to use the crutch when our
own legs (our own loves, tastes, habits etc.) can
do the journey on their own.

C. S. LEWIS

Back in high school I played basketball (all five foot four of me), and each summer we attended a camp as a team. With a new coach and a new year ahead, camp was our first and best opportunity to begin building unity, sharpening our skills, and growing as a cohesive unit.

I had an awesome first few days at camp! I was in the starting lineup every game, and the new coach seemed to like me. Plays came easily; I felt strong and in good physical shape. Until day three. During a rebound attempt, I came down and instantly fell to the floor. I had landed wrong and heard an ominous pop in my ankle. In a moment, my incredible week ended as I lay on the floor, crying out in agony. Perhaps the worst pain came from knowing that I probably wouldn't get to play much the rest of the week, and that my starting spot would now be in jeopardy.

The only encouraging thing (though now I see how silly it is) was the possibility of getting to use crutches. The best indication of a "real" battle wound around basketball camp was to be on crutches—it was almost like a status symbol. My ankle was huge, bruised, and extremely tender. I knew it had to be worse than a minor sprain, and I was glad when the first-aid worker agreed. But, after affirming my diagnosis, she gave me the next worst news of that week: I didn't need crutches.

What? I had to have them! This woman obviously didn't know the intensity of my pain or the severity of my injury (dramatic much?). Assuming everyone would think I was a wimp, I hobbled away frustrated—complete with damaged pride and a bubble-wrapped ankle.

If you talk to anyone who's ever had a *real* injury and had to have crutches for long periods of time, they'll tell you that crutches are horrible, and they certainly aren't a way of life. Crutches are an aid to help you heal, get stronger, and learn to walk again. They're never an end in themselves—they're a means to an end: health. The whole reason for having crutches is to get off them, which means you must use them for a time to develop the strength to stand on your own.

Here's the thing about healing from an injury: time will pass either way, whether you're on crutches or not. The only difference is how quickly and effectively you will heal. This is why people who want to reach maximum health *must* follow their doctor's orders to use crutches for a scheduled period of time. They must give their body time to strengthen, do the physical therapy to help the process, and exercise patience along the way.

The same is true for this book, which we call the 31-Day Pursuit Challenge. Thirty-one days will pass whether you read this book or not—and whether you apply its principles or not. The question is, how different will you be after that time? How different will your relationship with your husband be? How much deeper will your understanding of the gospel be?

Consider this book a crutch. And as C. S. Lewis pointed out, a crutch is a tool, not a substitute for what it supports. A tool like this can never replace your love for your husband, but it can help *strengthen* it and give it *time to grow*. In a perfect world—and if we were perfect women—we would never need a book like this to spur us along in the pursuit of our husbands. We'd readily love and pursue our husbands as we should and as they deserve: selflessly, consistently, joyfully, and in ways that connect most with their hearts. As you are likely well aware, the world is far from perfect, and it won't be until Jesus returns. Until then, we cling to hope, live with joy in him, and ravenously consume all the gospel-centered help and wisdom we can find!

THE PURSUIT CHALLENGE

Fierce wife, consider this your fair warning. The next thirty-one days won't be easy. That's why it's called a challenge! It's meant to stretch you. It will require new honesty with yourself and your husband. It will require work—*real effort*—that you might not want to do. And it will cost you time, energy, and cash (though how much is up to you). You will need fortitude and determination if you're going to finish this journey well. But it will be worth it!

There is an upside. I can assure you that your effort won't be in vain. If you apply yourself—*if you stay the course*—you will grow, your marriage will grow, and your husband will experience your love in new ways.

One particular verse has been pivotal for me while writing this book: "Commit your way to the LORD; trust in him and he will act" (Psalm 37:5). I can't guarantee this book will fix every broken area of your relationship or make it the absolute best marriage possible (what book can?). However, I can promise that it will point you to a Savior who is more than able to maximize your joy, restore hope, redeem difficult situations, and bring healing.

I don't recommend reading this book with ulterior motives of getting your husband to do something you want him to do or become someone you want him to be. This book is not about him, it's about you. It's about *your* heart. It's about you pursuing him purely, honestly, transparently, and confidently because of who you are in Christ. You may find that easy to do, or you may find it extremely hard. I've discovered that I can only pursue and love my husband well when I'm in constant relationship with Jesus and the gospel is at work in my own heart. Thus, that's the underlying premise for this entire book: a wife loves her husband best when she treasures Jesus most.

As you go through each of the next thirty-one days, your relationship with Jesus will grow. This book will require you to trust him, hold fast to his promises, and rest in the knowledge that

God is at work in you and your husband whether you see it at that moment or not. "Commit your way to the LORD," fierce wife, and trust him to act. He won't let you down.

GETTING THE MOST FROM THIS PROCESS

To get the most from this book, I encourage you to commit to this journey. Give yourself permission to spend the time and energy needed every day to get the most out of each one. Take time to read slowly through the Scriptures. Set aside intentional and undistracted moments to study and reflect. Do the good work of pursuit—of God and your husband. Pray, read, absorb, write, think, and act without reservation. Go all in; it's the only way. Finally, be honest with yourself, with God, and with your husband.

Let's get started on this journey together, my fierce friend! I'm excited to see God work in your life and in your marriage. To him be all the glory!

Stay fierce,

My Prayer for You

Lord, help this sweet wife live in light of your love, sacrifice, and gift of abundant life here on earth, and eternal life after this one. May she cling to you, and may her soul be quenched. May she continue to find rest, joy, and fulfillment in your holy presence. Fill her to overflowing with your love and new mercies throughout the next thirty-one days and beyond. May she come to you in her tiredness and be renewed by your Spirit. Help her experience the depths of your love and pursuit of her, and help her to pursue her husband out of a soul secure in you. Thank you for pursuing her heart. Lead her to do the same for her husband.

In Jesus' name I ask and believe. Amen.

Challenge Accepted

I, _____ , *accept this challenge.*

YOUR NAME

I understand that pursuing my husband won't always be easy, but he is always worth the fight.

I realize that it is only by God's grace that I am loved in Christ, and it will only be through God's grace that I grow and learn to love my husband as I am called.

Finally, I understand that my husband is a gift from God and it is my duty, honor, and privilege to love him for the rest of my life.

_____

SIGNATURE

_____

DATE

The 31 Day Pursuit
CHALLENGE

We love because
he first loved us.

1 JOHN 4:19

Before You Start

You may find it helpful to know how each day is structured:

SCRIPTURE

Every day starts with a passage from the Bible. Read it well. Nothing will transform your heart more than carefully reading God's Word and letting it read you.

DEVOTIONAL CONTENT

The devotionals draw connecting lines between the gospel and married life to help you discern the character and will of God, experience his love, and apply it to how you pursue your husband.

REFLECTION QUESTIONS

Each day includes a few questions to help you process the day's content and apply it to the pursuit challenge. The quality of your experience depends on how much effort you put in. Take time to answer honestly and thoroughly — it could pay off for years.

PRAYER

There are short prayer prompts to help get you started with

prayers of your own. I recommend writing a few short sentences of prayer each day in the space provided as a way of journaling your ongoing dialogue with God.

DAILY PURSUITS

The pursuit challenges are what make this experience unique. Each one is designed to help you pursue your husband in new ways. Some challenges are hard and involved, others are fast and fun. Resolve now to complete each one to the best of your ability.

ICONS

Each pursuit has icons to give you an idea of how much time and money you can expect to spend *relative to the other pursuits*. Exactly how much time and money you spend will always depend on you. They're suggestions, not requirements.

FIELD NOTES

This section is for jotting down any revelations, thoughts, or observations about how the pursuit went or how your husband responded. This will help you learn and improve for the future.

HEADS-UP!

You'll see *Heads-Up* prompts on some of the days. They allow you to plan for pursuits that are more involved. Heed them and it will go well with you. Remember: planning is part of the pursuit.

Most foundationally, marriage is the *doing* of God. And ultimately, marriage is the *display* of God.

JOHN PIPER

1

Pursuing Him as You Are Pursued

While we were still weak, at the right time Christ died for the ungodly. For one will scarcely die for a righteous person—though perhaps for a good person one would dare even to die—but God shows his love for us in that while we were still sinners, Christ died for us.

ROMANS 5:6–8

My wifely imperfections have a way of showing up... every... single... day. Whether I spend an entire day not saying anything kind, loving, or intentional to my husband, or treating him with a lack of respect or honor, I am constantly reminded of who I am apart from Christ. But it's in my failure that I am reminded and encouraged of how much God loves and pursues me, despite myself. Praise God that his knowledge of our shortcomings didn't slow him down in his pursuit of us. He knew the depth and entirety of our sins (past, present, and future) and he still chose to die. Why? Because he loves us. He *loves* us!

Do you know God's love? Have you *experienced* the truth of today's Scripture passage? God graciously continues to show me his love through his Word and through Christ's radical pursuit of my needy soul. That is good news that never gets old! The gospel is a message that can never be overstated. Why? Because it's only when we understand God's love and Christ's sacrifice in his pursuit of our hearts that we can fully and completely pursue our husbands.

If you're like me, you live to check items off the proverbial list. Pursuing your husband is not exactly a box you can check off your to-do list. Pursuit is a life attitude—one that ideally comes from of a place of joy. Not because of what your husband does or doesn't do, but because of our God who first loved and pursued us. If we are to pursue and love our husbands purely and confidently, our souls must find security in the Lord first. We must grasp the good news of how relentlessly we are pursued by Jesus, and that truth must transform our hearts.

It's tempting in a book like this to prescribe a list of steps for a better marriage: *Do more of this and that so your marriage looks and functions how it should.* But loving and pursuing your husband well doesn't start with your actions, it starts with your heart. It is true that you are called to love your husband in tangible, visible ways, but only as an overflow of how you're loved by Christ. It is the only way you can better love your husband. Christ's love always starts in you and flows outward through you.

In my pursuit of my husband, I can tell when I'm operating on my own strength instead of resting in the security of the gospel. How? My decisions and actions toward my husband are based on an unstated litany of "if-then" statements (*If* he does this, *then* I'll do that). Can you imagine if Christ kept a similar list? We'd all be in trouble! Thank God for Jesus and the gracious ways in which he pursues us. As it turns out, we need the exact same graciousness in marriage.

Today marks the start of your journey of learning how to pursue your husband more intentionally. But first, I need to be honest with you: I want this book to be more than a glorified list of ideas and to-dos. First and foremost I want you to finish the next thirty-one days with a deeper understanding of who Christ is and *who you are* as a result.

Second, I pray that as we journey deeper into Christ's profound love, we are transformed from the inside out, and that transformation dramatically affects how we love our husbands. I may have written this book, but I assure you that you and I are on this journey together.

Finally and most importantly, I want to remind you daily of the good news of Jesus. I've discovered that I need constant reminders of the gospel—even if I "know" it in my head. Because of that, you'll hear me talk about the gospel more than you might expect in a marriage devotional. That's because it's the *one thing* I (we) need to hear more than anything else. We *need* Jesus!

Once we're rooted in the gospel, we can better use practical tools to become more intentional wives. In the following days, I want to share that gospel and those tools with you. Onward!

REFLECT

How exactly has Christ loved and pursued you? List two or three specific ways.

In what ways do you foresee the gospel changing how you love and pursue your husband?

PRAY

Ask God to help you experience Jesus' reckless love for you in new ways, and pray for help remembering that the gospel is the "why" behind your actions.

Pursuit 1

ACT

Find and write down at least three verses that illustrate how you are loved and pursued by Christ. Explain in your own words how being pursued by Christ influences how you can pursue your husband.

____ *Check here when you've completed this pursuit.*

FIELD NOTES

Thoughts, feelings, or observations about today's pursuit?

HEADS-UP!

This may seem early, but it will be upon you in no time. Go ahead and take a peek at Day 31. It's not too soon to start planning!

2

Genuine Generosity

On the last day of the feast, the great day, Jesus stood up and cried out, "If anyone thirsts, let him come to me and drink. Whoever believes in me, as the Scripture has said, 'Out of his heart will flow rivers of living water.'"

JOHN 7:37–38

As a wife (and mother), it's easy to feel like I am always giving of myself day in and day out, with little or nothing left by the evening. Things to do, people to keep happy, and never enough time. It's emotionally, physically, mentally, and spiritually exhausting! By the end of the day I feel empty, thirsty, and reluctant to give any more of myself than the minimum requirement. How can I possibly pursue my husband generously when I feel *so* empty most of the time?

The answer, as with most things, is Jesus! He's the generous lover and pursuer of my soul, and the one who is abundantly enough for me. He sits patiently waiting for me to stop spinning my wheels in every direction and pursuing the things my soul longs for but can only be found in him. Through his Word he gently and lovingly pursues me and reminds me that he is my Living Water—that he is calling, "Come to me and drink." Not only that my deepest thirsts be quenched, but "out of [my] heart will flow living water." In an instant, he refreshes, moving me from thirsty to overflowing. From scarcity to abundance. That's quite a reversal!

Consider this permission to say "pass" to the pressure. Rest and trust that God is working and transforming your heart, even at this very moment. If and when you feel tired, weary, and parched, simply drink. Know that you have nothing more to prove; you need only run to Jesus and be washed away in his living waters. Then, trust him to work powerfully, miraculously, and diligently in you, through you, and around you.

Pursuing your husband becomes a delight rather than a burden when you are secure in Jesus. Joyfully giving of yourself completely and generously can be something you desire—not an obligation—because out of your heart will flow "rivers of living water."

My prayer for us as wives is that the Holy Spirit would be a constant helper to our souls, reminding and guiding us in the truth of the gospel. From there, I pray that our pursuits of our husbands would be marked by a generous flood of living water and everything it brings with it: love, grace, patience, hope, joy, appreciation, affection, and much, much more.

REFLECT

How do you treat your husband when you feel tired and depleted?
Are there ways you can improve?

What are three ways you can be more generous to your husband,
even when you don't feel up to the task?

PRAY

Ask God for an attitude of generosity that is rooted in Christ's
abundance and for help in understanding how to rest in Jesus.

ACT

⊙ ◔ ◑ | $ $ $

Today's pursuit is a symbolic gesture of a deeper truth. Give your husband a gift or do something generous *as* a gift. What you give or do doesn't have to have a price tag attached (it can), but it does need to be generous.

Explain to your husband what your generosity means: how you want to pursue him generously just as you have been pursued generously by Christ.

___ *Check here when you've completed this pursuit.*

FIELD NOTES

Thoughts, feelings, or observations about today's pursuit?

DAY

3

Ditch Distraction

Look carefully then how you walk, not as unwise but as wise,
making the best use of the time, because the days are evil.
Therefore do not be foolish, but understand
what the will of the Lord is.

EPHESIANS 5:15–17

Distraction is a human problem, not a technology problem. Screens are more readily available than ever before, but the battle against distraction is not new. It's also a timeless battleground in the fight for your marriage. For instance, we can now watch whatever show we want, whenever we want, and for as long as we want, all the while flipping through our various social media feeds in the process. If you're a real virtuoso, you might even have your laptop or tablet out so you can get some work done as well. Part of my heart longs for fewer distractions, but there's another part that feels a deep, incessant need for the attention, affirmation, and escape these distractions provide. The Enemy would love us to believe the lies that screen time costs us nothing and that distraction is harmless, especially as it pertains to our marriages. I assure you the opposite is true.

In today's Scripture verses, Paul was writing a letter to the Ephesian church, encouraging and instructing them to "make the best use of the time" by not being "foolish" and by understanding God's will. Now, I'm not saying that having Internet or social media accounts is against God's will, or even foolish (hello, blog writer here!). I am saying that, if left unchecked, the amount of time we spend on screens quickly becomes "foolish" as it steals our time, focus, and attention from what really matters.

So what should we be doing to make "the best use of the time" when it comes to our marriage and pursuing our husbands? Glad you asked! A few verses after today's passage, Paul gives us a clue. He instructs us to build each other up with "psalms and hymns and spiritual songs" (Ephesians 5:19). Those words have huge implications for marriage.

How many times have you (I'm also speaking to myself) spent the evening sitting around the house, TV on in the background, phones in hand, and just zoning out until it's time to go to bed? Wouldn't that time be better spent talking? What if you used those moments to dream, discuss Scripture, or encourage each other in the things of God? What if you spent that time playing a game or working on a small project together? The possibilities are vast, but you're probably starting to see the difference between "making the best use of the time" and being foolish with it.

As a wife, you can pursue your husband by recognizing

opportunities to make the best use of your time together, then lovingly initiating high-quality interaction. When you notice that you're not using your time well, stop and lovingly redirect your focuses elsewhere. Offer suggestions for activities you can do together that won't be wasteful. Go for an ice cream run, bust out a pack of playing cards, crack your Bibles, or think of a few interesting conversation prompts. You'd be surprised how quickly you both get distracted from your distractions!

On the flip side, it takes two, I get it. There are plenty of times when Ryan *wants* to be on his phone instead of playing a game or doing something that requires effort (and the same is true for me at times). You may not successfully kill distractions every time, but it's always wise to try.

In moments when it's tough to ditch distraction, you have a few options. First, you can give up trying and do whatever happens easiest. Second, you can insist on turning off devices, use an inflammatory tone, start an argument, then end up fighting instead of building your friendship (not sure if fighting is a "wise" use of time either). Or third, you can be loving and patient but intentional and persistent in your pursuit. Use caution not to let your persistence turn into nagging, or you'll find yourself in scenario two. If at first you don't succeed, try again the next day.

Whether ditching distraction happens easily in your marriage or it requires effort, it's worth it. You will never regret spending less time distracted, and every second you invest into building your marriage is certainly a wise and worthy use of your time.

REFLECT

Is distraction something you deal with often? What would you say distracts you the most?

Has technology (phone, TV, Internet) hindered your closeness with Jesus or your husband? If so, how? Be honest.

PRAY

Ask God for a new alertness toward unwise uses of your time. Pray for wisdom and conviction in areas that need to be surrendered to God, then ask for his help in doing so.

Pursuit 3

ACT

⊙⊙⊙ | $ $ $

Remove all distractions for an entire day or evening. Shut off your phones, turn off the TV, cancel activities, and see what happens! Get creative with what you do with the time. Try to do or talk about something brand new.

(If your husband is following his own 31-Day Pursuit Challenge on the same schedule, he'll be trying a similar pursuit today. Consider discussing what you learn and combining your efforts!)

___ *Check here when you've completed this pursuit.*

FIELD NOTES

Thoughts, feelings, or observations about today's pursuit?

HEADS-UP!

In two days you'll be playing your favorite game together. You may want to make sure you have it on hand.

DAY

4

The Wisest Words

She opens her mouth with wisdom,
and the teaching of kindness is on her tongue.

PROVERBS 31:26

For years I read Proverbs 31 and felt motivated and demoralized at the same time. I believed that the attributes of a godly woman it describes were an ultimate standard for me to strive for rather than something the gospel produces in my heart. I'm so grateful that Jesus pursued my mind and helped me better understand this important, beautiful passage.

While Proverbs 31 outlines a good set of qualities for women to match, it's not *primarily* written to urge us toward that standard. As Ryan often reminds me, "it's *descriptive* rather than *prescriptive*." It shows us what a godly woman is like, not what we need to be like in order to become godly. The woman the chapter describes is someone who loves God, carries herself with wisdom, and possesses all the traits of a woman secure in her identity as a daughter of God. This was a huge paradigm shift for me. The life of a woman of God is indeed one of becoming like the Proverbs 31 woman, except the becoming happens because of heart transformation, not behavior modification.

Today's verse describes one trait of a Proverbs 31 woman that Christ wants to produce in me: the ability to open my mouth with wisdom. God is transforming how I speak to my husband. All too often tension arises between us because I either use too many words, try to use fewer words and end up blowing up because I bottled them up, or use words as a weapon to hurt and tear him down. Words have always been a challenge for me, but by God's grace that is changing.

God continues to remind me of his intention for my words as a wife speaking to my husband. I'm learning what it means to let wisdom and kindness flow out of me in the heat of a frustrating moment (despite my feelings). I'm also learning the peace of knowing I no longer have to justify myself—or feel vindicated—through what I say and how I say it. I can rest knowing I am justified and vindicated in Christ.

Knowing my identity doesn't just help me keep my mouth shut, it also compels me to speak life when it's needed. I am free to "open [my] mouth with wisdom" and have "the teaching of kindness" on my tongue in ways that help my husband. I'm forever grateful that thanks to Christ, I have nothing more to prove!

Fierce wife, what you say matters. Know *whose* you are, and let your identity in Christ fuel your every word.

REFLECT

Recall a time when someone was generous with you with their words. How did that make you feel?

How can you use wise and kind words to intentionally honor and pursue your husband? What can you say to him that will encourage him most?

PRAY

Give thanks to God for transforming you into the woman described in Proverbs 31. Pray for wisdom and kindness in your words to your husband and for the Holy Spirit to convict you when your words are hurtful.

ACT

⊙⊙⊙ | $ $ $

Pursue him through intentionally generous words. Write a letter to read out loud to him, outlining three things you are most grateful for in him.

Consider highlighting how he leads your family, how hard he works, ways he loves you, or how he sacrifices his needs and wants for your family. Be as articulate as you can. Take some undistracted time to sit, pray, and write.

Read your letter to him at some point today.

___ *Check here when you've completed this pursuit.*

FIELD NOTES

Thoughts, feelings, or observations about today's pursuit?

5

The Best Medicine

A joyful heart is good medicine,
but a crushed spirit dries up the bones.

PROVERBS 17:22

Ryan taught me how to play chess when we were dating. Well, he tried once . . . but I found it frustrating and uninteresting at the time. After we got married, though, he patiently explained it to me a few more times, and it has since become one of our favorite games; except, he usually wins. Card games, however, are a different story; I always win those!

Ryan enjoys playing games and often initiates a round. Admittedly, I'm reluctant at first but always glad I played in the end. We're both competitive, and we've discovered that we laugh a lot whenever we take the time to play a game together.

Aside from the gospel, nothing brings Ryan and me closer than laughter, and nothing gets us laughing quite like playing games together. Perhaps a joyful heart truly is "good medicine," as today's verse says?

Have you ever wondered why "good medicine" is used in Proverbs 17:22 instead of something else? Why not "good steak"? Steak tastes good, and it provides protein and minerals to your body once eaten. Surely eating a good steak would make for a similar comparison to the good benefits of a "joyful heart." Maybe Solomon was driving at something a little deeper than just feeling better for a time?

A joyful heart is not something we're wired to fake. It must be genuine. And when medicine is consumed, it's not for general nutrition, but for a purpose—to treat a sickness. For followers of Christ, a joyful heart is as sure as his finished work on the cross—our eternal infirmity has been cured. Nothing will shake it and no one can remove it. However, we're human beings living in an imperfect world, so our joy isn't always felt. By uplifting your spirit (as opposed to having a "crushed spirit"), you awaken your deep joy and in doing so, take your "good medicine."

There will be moments when your spirit feels crushed. There will be times when your marriage feels dry. It's in those times that you can awaken your deep joy by stirring your hope in Jesus, resting in his accomplished work on the cross, and having some fun—a "joyful heart"—with your husband in light of it all.

Laughter and fun are good, gracious gifts from God. Today's pursuit is about remembering those gifts and making time to enjoy them with your best friend. Fierce wife, partake of the joy that is yours in Christ; doing so will always bring health and life to your marriage.

REFLECT

What is the most fun you've ever had with your husband? Briefly describe what happened.

What about that experience made it particularly enjoyable?

PRAY

Ask God for a renewed and refreshed sense of fun in your heart and in your marriage.

Pursuit 5

ACT

⊙ ⊙ ⊙ | $ $ $

Pick a game you both enjoy and play it this evening. If you don't own the game, borrow it from a friend. If you don't have a favorite game, try something new together!

___ *Check here when you've completed this pursuit.*

FIELD NOTES

Thoughts, feelings, or observations about today's pursuit?

HEADS-UP!

In two days you're tasked with relieving your husband of one routine duty he usually takes care of. Keep an eye out for ideas of things you can do.

DAY

6

Selfless, Intentional Affection

We have come to know and to believe the love that God has for us. God is love, and whoever abides in love abides in God, and God abides in him.

I JOHN 4:16

Honesty time: if Ryan and I don't intentionally stop and hug or kiss each other, affection just won't happen. Life gets so fast-paced and hectic that we simply forget. It definitely takes more of a conscious effort on my part because physical touch isn't the number-one way that I feel close or connected to my husband. However, I know that when I take the time to hug or kiss him, rub the back of his neck while we're in the car, or grab his hand while we're walking, it always speaks volumes to him. His *heart* hears it, his whole being feels it, and all at once his love bucket fills up. If we weren't connecting before, suddenly we are. As a result he often reciprocates with the types of affection he knows

I enjoy most. It's a win-win! I've found that when I step out in faith—in God and in my husband—it softens our hearts, connects us, and multiplies our affection. But it definitely goes against my flesh at times.

To be honest, this type of pursuit isn't easy; I used to never pursue my husband with affection unless I felt like showing him affection. But something in me changed.

I've discovered that the more I understand Christ's love for me, the less my own preferences matter. If I stop to think about what it means to have been pursued by Christ in my sin, it still blows my mind (Romans 5:6, 8). Talk about selflessness and intentionality! Jesus engaged in a loving, radical pursuit of my soul, knowing all my faults—past, present, and future—but it wasn't enough to stop him. Abiding in his love and the message of the gospel compels me to be intentionally affectionate toward my husband in ways that speak to him. It doesn't matter how my husband responds, I can still choose to show him love. Don't get me wrong, I *want* my husband to respond well to affection, but his reaction doesn't ultimately determine my decision to love, Christ does.

So be brave, make the effort, and reach out. Let's be selfless and intentional about pursuing our husbands in ways that communicate to them. If being affectionate is challenging for you, I encourage you to take at least one step today, no matter how small. Even the smallest intentional acts of love have a way of shattering walls, building closeness, and multiplying love in a marriage.

REFLECT

What are your husband's favorite displays of affection?

What daily opportunities can you identify for showing him love in ways he hears best?

PRAY

Ask God to lead and guide you in how to confidently pursue your husband through affection.

Pursuit 6

ACT

⏱ ⏱ ⏱ | $ $ $

Identify two ways you plan to show affection physically to your husband—and then make it happen.

Keep in mind that loving affection doesn't have to include sex. However, if that's where it goes naturally, have fun!

___ *Check here when you've completed this pursuit.*

FIELD NOTES

Thoughts, feelings, or observations about today's pursuit?

DAY
7

Sweet, Sweet Relief

Therefore he had to be made like his brothers in every respect, so that he might become a merciful and faithful high priest in the service of God, to make propitiation for the sins of the people.

HEBREWS 2:17

It's easy to become too task oriented. Too many times I let my ever-growing to-do list become the driver of my decisions, attitudes, and behavior toward my husband. I can grow too focused on what I have to do, what I've done, and how my husband hasn't contributed to my day's productivity (hey, I'm not saying it's accurate—it's just how I start to feel). The side of me that demands justice often defaults to anger, which means my tone starts to bite, my words get snippier, and I my angry train of thought goes completely off the rails. In my task-oriented fog ,it's so easy for me to point out everything he didn't do that day. However, if I were to take a step back and maybe even walk a few steps in his shoes, I might realize there's more happening than I initially thought, and he has an entire world of work he's dealing with himself.

My husband does things—*a lot of things*—every day that go unnoticed and unappreciated. It's hard to see everything he does for me and our family when I'm utterly consumed by my own concerns. Instead of seeing, appreciating, acknowledging, and loving my husband for what he does, I pridefully assume I'm carrying most of the weight around the Frederick household and insist on "setting the record straight." Alternatively, I should be trying to understand, to empathize, and to perceive his value for our family. Sigh. Thank God for Christ's example once again.

How grateful I am for a Savior who isn't ignorant to our circumstances. Today's verse says Jesus "had to be made like his brothers in every respect, so that he might become a merciful and faithful high priest." Once again, Christ proves to us the lengths to which he has gone to love us, or as the passage puts it, "to make propitiation for the sins of the people."

Did Jesus have to endure suffering to know what suffering was like? Being that he's omniscient (all-knowing), I don't believe so. However, Hebrews does say that, "because he himself has suffered when tempted, he is able to help those who are being tempted" (2:18). Our God so loved his people that he became one of us so he could help us. Let that sink in a bit. That's love. And that's the clearest picture of pursuit I can possibly imagine.

So, here *I* am, a wife who gets mad if I've done dishes more than my fair share over the past few days! Lord help me. If we can learn anything from today's verse, it's this: we have a Savior who understands our temptations, our struggles, and can "sympathize with our weaknesses" (Hebrews 4:15). How much more can we learn to sympathize with our husband's workload, stresses, and tiredness?

A large part of pursuit means putting yourself in your husband's shoes and seeking to understand his perspective. You may not be able to fill in for him at work for the day, but you can certainly get curious, ask questions, and make a concerted effort to observe his contribution to your household.

Chances are, you are already grateful for everything your husband does, and that's good! Today's pursuit is about deepening your understanding and communicating exactly what you're thankful for directly to your husband. Nothing begets joy quite like gratitude, and few things can fill your husband with joy like authentically expressing your gratitude to him for everything he does for you.

REFLECT

What duties does your husband do that you couldn't do without?

Which do you most appreciate, and why?

PRAY

Thank and praise God for the many ways your husband helps out. Ask God for clarity and direction on how you can bring sweet relief to your husband.

Pursuit 7

ACT

⊙⊙◌ | $ $ $

Release your husband from one duty he routinely handles. Your goals are to understand his perspective a little more and to express gratitude for what he does.

Pick a chore he usually does or a small house project he'd normally take care of, your call. If you're stumped, just ask! Either way, express your gratitude for what he does for you and your family, and explain why you're covering one of his duties for the day.

___ *Check here when you've completed this pursuit.*

FIELD NOTES

Thoughts, feelings, or observations about today's pursuit?

HEADS-UP!

Clear your calendar for tomorrow evening, since tomorrow's pursuit involves getting intimate.

8

Love Pursues Intimacy

The watchmen found me as they went about in the city.
"Have you seen him whom my soul loves?"

SONG OF SOLOMON 3:3

Sex is a beautiful gift designed by God exclusively for marriage. It is a physical expression of a *spiritual commitment* to loving the whole person for life. When you're naked with your husband, it's a beautiful representation of unity and intimacy that ideally should exist in every level of your lives. As wives, we want to be desired sexually by our husbands, but not primarily or exclusively in that way. We want to know they want *all* of us, not just our bodies. (Sidenote: If you and your husband are reading both 31-Day Pursuit books together, rest assured—Ryan has written to them on this topic today as well.)

Generally speaking, most men desire sex more than their wives, though that's not always the case. It seems to be the case for Ryan and me. That sometimes means that as the wife, my tendency is to feel steamrolled in the bedroom, or even pressured into having sex (though that's not the reality). This raises the question: How do wives pursue their husbands sexually without feeling like they are offering themselves up solely as a means to his physical satisfaction?

Since it would be unhelpful and unwise for me to assume I know how sex works in your marriage, let's explore two universal truths about sex that apply no matter the situation. Doing so will hopefully provide clarity on how wives can better love and pursue their husbands through sex.

First, sex is always *exclusive*. It's isolated to you, your husband, and your marriage. Nothing from the outside should invade or contaminate your sexual experience, and your desire should be for your husband—for *all* of him and *only* him. The goal of sexual pursuit is not only physical pleasure, but rather a deeper bond—a mutual experience of complete, unhindered, and uncontaminated intimacy. Part of keeping sex exclusive means leaving all distractions, expectations, agendas, and pre-established ideas at the door. This frees you and your husband to focus on the same goal: each other. Sex is about knowing who he is to you and loving him deeply; body to body, soul to soul.

Second, sex always requires *intentional communication*. Ryan and I have established (through many misfires and arguments) what we call the "Spectrum of Sex." It's basically the idea that not all sex is the same, and that's to be expected. Sometimes sex is passionate and intense, and other times it's fast and functional.

Both "formats" are edifying, just as long as you're on the same page. Having an agreed-upon idea of what sex can be like for us helps us avoid missed expectations and their resulting arguments. For example, before getting frisky, we usually have a quick chat about what's feasible given how much time we have (e.g. the kids are napping), how tired we are, and what mood we're both in. This clears the air and helps us find agreement. If we each have a similar idea of what to expect, we can experience unity and grow in intimacy regardless of what the specific act of sex entails that time.

So today's challenge of pursuing intimacy with your husband might be a little tricky because sex is a loaded topic for many couples. Also, you both want to have honest and pure motives without pressuring each other. The solution? Total vulnerability and honesty with where you're at and what your (selfless) expectations are for this time together.

As a wife, you know your husband better than anyone. How does your husband feel most satisfied (on every level: emotionally, spiritually, physically) before, during, and after sex? How can you *pursue* him sexually? It's helpful to remember that *he* is your goal—his soul. Just like the woman in the passage above who dreamt about pursuing the one her soul loves, let your husband be the one your soul deeply loves and fiercely desires.

REFLECT

What part of intimacy makes your husband feel most desired?
Be specific.

Do you find sex mostly enjoyable or mostly challenging? Why?

PRAY

Ask God how you can pursue your husband's heart from a place
of honesty and confidence. Thank him for the good gift of sex
and pray for a new/renewed appreciation for it.

ACT   ☻☻☺ | $ $ $

Initiate intimacy and sex. Set the stage by planning ahead (especially if you have kids) and creating a romantic atmosphere. Consider turning on some music or lighting a candle, or perhaps something more involved like a surprise night away when you've packed something sexy to wear. Plan to put into action whatever speaks to your husband the most so he feels like you're pursuing him without distraction.

(If your husband is going through his own 31-Day Pursuit Challenge, rest assured that he'll be reading about the same thing. He'll be "setting the stage" as well. Consider discussing how you can work together to make it an incredible evening.)

___ *Check here when you've completed this pursuit.*

FIELD NOTES

Thoughts, feelings, or observations about today's pursuit?

Real love, the Bible says, instinctively desires permanence.

TIMOTHY KELLER

9

Gracious, Sweet Familiarity

Gracious words are like a honeycomb,
sweetness to the soul and health to the body.

PROVERBS 16:24

I first met Ryan in the eighth grade. He had come to our school as a visitor with a mutual friend. He was quiet, had blonde-tipped (bleached) hair, baggy pants, a chain attached to his wallet, braces, and a big ugly T-shirt with Mr. Potato Head on it. Oh, and he had no discernible personality whatsoever (he'd agree, by the way). He was incredibly shy and based on what I saw, I wondered if he ever talked to anyone.

It's funny to reminisce about what we thought about each other when we first met and how much we've both changed since then. Over the years our affection has grown—but so has our familiarity, which can be both good and challenging.

Familiarity is a mixed blessing in marriage. There are two very different sides to the same coin. On one side, as I've grown closer to my husband it has allowed me to be vulnerable with him more quickly, more easily, and on deeper levels than with anyone else. On the other side, I can't tell you how many times I've been *too* familiar, which has caused me to grow lazy in our relationship. This laziness typically translates into poor tone choice and nitpicking, nagging, or frustration for whatever reason. Instead of reining in my feelings of anger or frustration toward him, I'll often let loose because . . . after all, *it's Ryan.*

When I let familiarity run rampant, my heart grows hard and pretty soon, my gratefulness for who he is and what he does for our family goes completely out the window. It makes me lose sight and forget what makes my husband remarkable. I forget all of his traits that drew me to him in the first place. And perhaps most tragically, I lose sight of just how special my husband is in God's eyes.

No one is more familiar with your husband—*or you*—than God. He knitted you together in your mother's womb (Psalm 139:13–16), he knows the number of hairs on your head (Luke 12:7), and he knows exactly what you do, think, say, and intend *every* moment of *every* day. Nothing about you is a mystery or a surprise to God! Yet, he is full of forgiveness and abounding in love. And, despite how much you neglect him, he stands ready to meet you wherever you are and pour out every one of his promises without delay. In Christ, we have all the benefits of familiarity without any of the drawbacks. That's what it means to be called daughter or child of God; that's the gospel!

In today's passage, Solomon reminds us of the power of gracious words. He says they're like honeycomb, adding "sweetness to the soul and health to the body." If we're not careful, familiarity can steal the graciousness of our words and rob our marriages of their sweetness and health. But on the flip side, if we're *mindful* and *wise*, our words can multiply the health in our marriages and ensure the enduring sweetness of our familiarity. Let's explore.

Gracious words are sweet to the soul because they echo the eternal graciousness of Christ into the trenches of everyday life. For example, when a wife chooses to forego an opportunity to "be right" and instead, chooses to speak with love, it breathes life into her husband and health into her marriage. But the effects of gracious words don't stop there.

Every infusion of gracious words has a multiplying effect—in your heart and in your husband's. Gratitude inevitably wells up inside you as love motivates your actions. Your husband feels your sweetness, love softens his heart, and he is more likely to reciprocate. The cycle continues, and your familiarity actually *fuels* your intimacy and closeness instead of sabotaging it.

Fierce wife, familiarity is a blessing that must be guarded and kept from growing bitter. Fight to keep your familiarity sweet. Remember the gift your husband is, and never lose sight of the person God created him to be. Then, with a heart fueled by the gospel and motivated by love, let your words flood your marriage with grace—adding sweetness to your husband's soul and health to your marriage.

REFLECT

In what ways have you experienced both sides of familiarity in your marriage?

How can you speak gracious words to your husband regularly? Provide at least three tangible examples.

PRAY

Ask God to help you to see your husband through his (God's) eyes. Pray for a genuine attitude of gratefulness.

Pursuit 9

ACT   ☉☉☉ | $ $ $

Carve out at least thirty minutes to spend some undistracted and intentional time with God. During this time, seek what God's Word says about who your husband is. Afterward, share it with your husband, speaking gracious, life-giving words over him.

You can start with these verses:

1.) _____ is loved by God (1 John 4:10–12). How does this affect my perspective of him?

2.) _____ is forgiven in Christ (Colossians 1:13–14). How does this deepen my grace toward him?

3.) _____ is the head (Ephesians 5:23). In light of the gospel, what response should this elicit from my heart toward him?

4.) _____ is valuable, body and soul (1 Corinthians 6:19–20). How does this knowledge affect how I treat my husband?

___ *Check here when you've completed this pursuit.*

FIELD NOTES

Thoughts, feelings, or observations about today's pursuit?

HEADS-UP!

On Day 11, you'll be having a new experience. Depending on what you decide to do, you may want a head start on planning!

DAY

10

Infusing Confidence

*Do nothing from selfish ambition or conceit, but in humility
count others more significant than yourselves.*

PHILIPPIANS 2:3

It took Ryan and me two years of friendship before we finally had our DTR (Define The Relationship) talk. While we knew each other, I didn't fully *notice* him until he came back from summer vacation: braces off, football physique, normal clothes, hair that was finally one color (not two), and a brain full of amazing thoughts he finally decided to share in our English class. I was hooked. I was also slightly heartbroken when he asked another girl to homecoming (this was before our talk). Apparently he thought I was out of his league, and I thought he just wasn't that into me. Needless to say, we found our way to each other.

One of my favorite things about our early dating relationship was the notes. Remember, this was before texting, and cell phones were far less advanced. It may sound archaic, but pen and paper was the best way to communicate. (I think it still is, by the way.) We would pass notes to each other in the hallways while walking between classes, or give each other a high five on the way into the room if we shared a class. He'd often hold my hand just *a little bit longer* and make my heart skip a few beats. (We went to a Christian school, so PDA was definitely not encouraged.)

Even back then, Ryan had a way with pen and paper. He works hard at writing and communicating well, but he also has a gift. He's always been able to encourage me and speak to me in a way that no one else can. I can't tell you how many times he's encouraged me in my faith or explained clearly how the gospel applies in circumstances or relationships where I am struggling to apply it. No one has a direct line to my heart quite like he does. He'd say the same about me.

God has taught me, through my many missed and failed attempts, that as a wife, I have unique access into my husband's heart. The question is, what do I do with it? Do I wield my heart access with "selfish ambition or conceit" as today's passage warns against, or do I count him more significant than myself, and use my access to serve him in love?

Words of encouragement speak volumes to me and are more my love language than Ryan's—this is why our notes meant so much to me. He's different. As I mentioned, he feels the most encouraged through an affectionate touch. When I grab his hand, or stop him in the middle of our kitchen and just hug him randomly, it encourages him and fills his bucket. He loves when I pursue him physically. It softens his heart, makes him feel loved, and deepens our connection. It's a no-brainer, right? Show him affection selflessly and he'll feel loved. . . I wish I could say I always followed my own advice!

It's hard to admit, but I don't always steward my access to my husband's heart as well as I would like. Instead of edifying him by speaking to him in ways that encourage his soul, my flesh would rather pursue him *my* way. I suppose it's a little like giving him a limited edition boxed set of the *Complete Works of Jane Austen* as a gift for Christmas. He might *see* the value, but it's just not something he's into. It's a selfish gift—which is actually an oxymoron!

Paul's above words to the Philippians carried profound purpose when he wrote them, and they still do today. He understood that the only way to live in loving, authentic community was to love each other selflessly in light of Christ's work on the cross. He knew that selfish love wasn't love at all, and that gospel-centered humility always multiplies life, joy, and love between believers.

That same principle beckons to us today. Will we, as wives, love our husbands selflessly and in ways that encourage them most? Will we trust Christ to *be our significance* as we count others—our husbands—more significant than ourselves?

Fierce wife, God has prepared and equipped you for this role, and because of him, you can confidently step into it. Use your access to your husband's heart to strengthen and remind him of the God you serve, his promises in Christ, and your husband's identity as an adopted son of God.

REFLECT

What type(s) of encouragement and love speak to your husband most? Do you find any of them challenging to give?

How can you give your husband more of the encouragement he enjoys most? How can you be more selfless in doing so?

PRAY

Ask God for insight into ways you can encourage your husband and for sureness of God's grace and sufficiency every step of the way.

ACT

⊙⊙⊙ | $ $ $

Think about the following questions:

1.) Lately, how have I been stewarding this "direct access" to my husband's heart?

2.) What challenges is he facing that require courage?

3.) How can I encourage and help strengthen him?

4.) What timely words will speak most to him?

Consider ways your words (as his wife) can infuse him with confidence. Text him (or give him a note) with these three things: a few words of encouragement, a prayer over him, and one verse meant to strengthen him.

___ *Check here when you've completed this pursuit.*

FIELD NOTES

Thoughts, feelings, or observations about today's pursuit?

11

Friendship and New Adventures

Oil and perfume make the heart glad, and the sweetness of a friend comes from his earnest counsel.

PROVERBS 27:9

People often ask us how we've stuck together all this time and still kept our marriage fun and fresh. With the exception of Jesus and the gospel (which is a *huge* exception), I would have to say that our friendship is the key. Through our friendship God initially brought us together, and through our friendship he has allowed and blessed us to make new memories and experiences together. All my greatest life memories have been with my husband.

Ryan is definitely my favorite person. No one makes me laugh as hard as he does, and no one has proven to be a more steadfast and worthy friend to me than he has. Having reached the point in life where Ryan and I have been together longer than we have been apart (including our married and dating years), I can confidently say that there is no one I would rather experience the highs and lows of marriage and life with than him.

In today's passage, Solomon compares friendship to fragrant oils and perfumes. Solomon says, "The sweetness of a friend comes from his earnest counsel." Essential oils immediately come to mind—have you ever smelled a bottle of quality essential oils? It's uncanny how potent that stuff is! One whiff, and the smell seems to linger in your nose for hours. It's usually a pleasant smell, so I tend not to mind.

Friendship is like that. It's pleasantly persistent and fiercely fragrant. It penetrates every aspect of your marriage and, like a strong fragrance, its presence is undeniable. We often associate friendship with having fun, but fun is just the beginning. Friends provide earnest counsel by giving timely, thoughtful, and diligent advice for life's big questions. True friends stand by each other during difficult seasons. They comfort one another without time line or agenda. They speak the truth in love, never holding back but always communicating in ways that are edifying. In short, a true friend values you for *who* you are, not what you can do for them.

Your friendship with your husband is foundational to your marriage. It's irreplaceable. There are no shortcuts to building an authentic friendship—it requires time, investment, and desire. That's what today's challenge is all about: building your friendship. Do the good work of cultivating genuine friendship with your husband. Laugh, cry, spend time, and create memories together. Each moment and every dollar is a worthy investment.

REFLECT

How has your husband been a friend to you? Think about the best ways you've been friends to each other.

What activities build your friendship most? List a few.

PRAY

Ask God for increased warmth and a deepening of friendship between you and your husband.

ACT

☺☺☺ | $$$

Plan a new experience with your husband and surprise him with it. Be creative! It need not be expensive (though it's fine if it is), but it must be something new that neither of you have ever done. Either set a date, plan it for today, or create a coupon for one new experience (redeemable in the next few weeks). Whatever you choose to do, don't delay! Plan something, do it, and make a new memory.

P.S. One of our first dates was at a park in Seattle (more on this later). We were picking blackberries (not new) along the waterfront, and somehow we got into a blackberry fight and fell in the lake (new!). We ended up having to change into our swimsuits because our regular clothing was wet. Just an example of something small, memorable, and new!

____ *Check here when you've completed this pursuit.*

FIELD NOTES

Thoughts, feelings, or observations about today's pursuit?

12

Knowing What You Don't Know

Every good gift and every perfect gift is from above, coming down from the Father of lights, with whom there is no variation or shadow due to change.

JAMES 1:17

It's embarrassing to admit, but I'm pretty naïve about slang. New phrases (new to me, anyway) often come up in a movie or TV show, and I'll have to ask Ryan what on earth they're talking about. My confused look makes him giggle—and if I venture to try whatever word or phrase I've just learned, it gives him a good gut laugh every time. We jokingly blame each other's upbringing: mine being "sheltered" and his being . . . well, not so sheltered.

Despite our many years together, I am still learning new things from him and *about* him. For example, I recently discovered that he doesn't actually know how to spell his own middle name. (It's crazy I know, but it's true.) I learned that *minor* tidbit just a few weeks back!

Ryan also teaches me things I didn't know about *myself*. For example, when I'm trying to keep an upcoming surprise from him, he always finds out beforehand. I had no idea how until he shared a secret with me: all he has to do is ask me a few questions and my facial expressions give it away. Specifically, my nostrils flare when I'm trying to keep a secret. I never knew that about myself until Ryan told me. That's just one example. I've learned countless truths about myself—about my personality, my identity in Christ, and even my own preferences—all through talking and processing life with him.

It's easy for married people to assume we know all there is to know about each other. The reality is that you both change—a lot! Interests change, beliefs are refined, priorities shift, and your personalities evolve. Even couples who have been married for fifty years admit to learning new things about their spouses regularly. This is because life is in constant flux: circumstances, people, and countless other factors all contribute to how we develop and adapt as individuals. As the old adage goes, "The only unchanging thing in life is change itself."

As followers of Christ, we can agree that everything and everyone changes. . . except God. As James wrote in today's verse, with the Father "there is no variation or shadow due to change." We can have complete assurance that no matter how much we change or how far life shifts, God *never* changes. He is the same God today that he was during creation. He will be the same God in a million years that he is today. Praise God!

Let this sink in: the unchanging, good, and gracious God of the Bible saw fit to give "every good gift and perfect gift" to us, an imperfect people prone to change (James 1:17). Now, that's pursuit. Even in light of eternity—which he sees in full view, outside of time—God sent his Son to die so we can be reconciled with him. But he doesn't stop with our reconciliation; as James said, every good gift comes from God. Beyond the gift of Jesus—our salvation—he showers believers with joy, peace, hope, and love. He provides for our needs (Philippians 4:19), and he graciously allows fulfillment of some of our wants. And finally for you, a wife, he has given you a husband—one of God's most obvious blessings in your life.

My husband is a good gift from God. He's multifaceted, complex, and ever changing. He is not the same man today that he will be in a year, nor is he the same man he was when we got married. Even more, God is as much at work in your husband as he is in you! One of the best ways you can pursue your husband is by seeing him for who he is today and embracing how God will change him tomorrow.

All too often I find myself so concerned with my own "stuff" that I stop seeing Ryan; I miss who he is and what God is doing in his heart. But whenever I take a step back from my own stuff to watch what God is doing in Ryan's heart, God softens my own heart and takes the focus off me.

So, how do I actually observe how my husband is changing? By engaging in intentional conversations with him, observing him (not in a creepy way) throughout his days and weeks, and by keeping an ear open for when he shares what God is teaching him. You can learn a lot about someone just by engaging, watching, and listening.

As for intentional conversations, make a point to go further than "How was your day?" Get specific. Pursue your husband's mind and heart by asking open-ended questions about what he thinks. Take an active interest in God's ongoing work in your husband's life. You will spend your entire life getting to know the man God gave you. Enjoy the journey, stay curious, and remember that every new discovery is a fresh opportunity to love him as Christ loved you.

REFLECT

What have been the most surprising things you've learned about your husband in the past?

What are a few open-ended questions you can ask your husband with the sole intent of learning something new about him?

PRAY

Ask God for wisdom and sensitivity in knowing your husband's heart. Pray for clear eyes to see him consistently as a gift, not a task on your to-do list.

Pursuit 12

ACT

🕐🕑🕒 | $ $ $

Spend today (one day) observing your husband and noting what he does and why. For example, if he is as consistent as the rising sun, why? What is it about him that likes consistency or doesn't? Take note of three things you have learned about him during the day and write them down.

Ask your husband about his favorite childhood memory with a parent or mentor. Why was it his favorite? What about it does he remember specifically (sights, smells, sounds, etc.), and why? If the conversations leads this way, share one of your favorite memories as well. Note one or two things you didn't know about him before this story.

_____ *Check here when you've completed this pursuit.*

FIELD NOTES

Thoughts, feelings, or observations about today's pursuit?

HEADS-UP!

You'll be asked to set aside a good chunk of time for an honest conversation with your husband on Day 14. Make sure you both have at least an hour of undistracted time available.

DAY
13

Serving Is Pursuing

*When he had washed their feet and put on his outer garments
and resumed his place, he said to them, "Do you understand
what I have done to you? You call me Teacher and Lord, and
you are right, for so I am. If I then, your Lord and Teacher, have
washed your feet, you also ought to wash one another's feet. For I
have given you an example, that you also should do
just as I have done to you.*

JOHN 13:12–15

Jesus presented a beautiful and deep picture of service when he washed his disciples' feet. At first glance we assume that Jesus was simply calling his followers to serve others—and that's part of what he was showing us, but I believe there's more. We can learn at least three key truths from Jesus' washing of the disciples' feet, and each one offers incredible implications for how you can pursue your husband.

The first truth we witness is that Jesus' actions foreshadowed his ultimate act of servanthood through death on the cross. In ancient culture, feet were very filthy and particularly exposed during meals as people reclined at low tables. The washing of feet before meals was a necessary practice! John was very intentional in describing how Jesus prepared to wash his disciples' feet: "He laid aside his outer garments, and taking a towel, tied it around his waist" (John 13:4). He then used that towel to wipe their feet dry after washing. Why did John include that last part about the towel? Wouldn't readers *assume* he'd have a towel? Or is there more? It could be said that Jesus' removal of his outer garment (his robe or mantle) and attaching the towel to his waist signified the removal of his divine mantle (his role in heaven) and donning humanity for the work to come on the cross. Jesus took on the sin of the world and now covers believers with his righteousness (2 Corinthians 5:21), much like he dirtied the towel with the disciples' foot filth and covered it with his outer garment once again. (John never mentions him removing the towel.)

The second truth we witness is that Jesus was opposing the proud attitudes of the disciples. In Luke's parallel account of the same story, the disciples fought over who would be regarded as the greatest (22:24). Jesus' example of humility and service would have shocked them in that moment. *How could he, their Teacher, stoop to such a level?* Jesus used his own example to remind them that "the leader is one who serves" (v. 26). In God's economy, the greatest are the least, the richest are the poorest, and the last shall be first. He was opposing their proud attitudes and refocusing them on what matters most to God.

The third truth is that Jesus reminded his disciples to follow his example by serving each other. As they sat down to eat, there were no servants in sight who could wash their feet. Still, it didn't occur to any of them to step in and serve their brothers in that way. Instead they just sat idle. As I mentioned, washing feet wasn't a formality or a nicety; it was a required prerequisite to a sanitary meal! To refuse to wash each other's feet would have been to say, "I'd rather not eat than do that!" There's a good chance the notion of washing the others' feet occurred to one of them, but clearly, no one acted on it. Jesus' example is a potent reminder that we're called to get our hands dirty by serving others, and we shouldn't allow pride or forgetfulness to get in the way.

I'm sure you can see the parallels here with how you can pursue your husband. As his wife, you can model Christ on the cross by serving freely, selflessly, and sacrificially. You get the opportunity to exemplify Jesus' love through serving your husband. Not in a way that assumes you're less than him (because you're not—and we're all made in the image of God). But rather, you can serve him in a way that reflects your heart being anchored in the knowledge of who you are *in* and *because of* Jesus.

To us the act of washing feet is symbolic, but it's also vivid. Shocking, even. Just as Jesus' example caught his disciples by surprise, you're likely to shock your husband when you begin actively pursuing him through radical, selfless service.

REFLECT

Reread and reflect on today's Scripture. What are your thoughts? Feelings? Why?

Is mutual service a regular part of your marriage? Why or why not?

PRAY

Ask God for an increased heart of servanthood toward your husband, and for wisdom in what that looks like.

Pursuit 13

ACT

⊙⊙⊙ | $ $ $

Today's challenge might make you a tad uncomfortable, but that's all right. This evening, take the time to wash each other's feet. Have him sit in a comfortable chair, grab a bowl, some water, and a towel. Explain to him about Jesus' example of loving-kindness through servanthood, and how you're learning to pursue him in the same way. I encourage you to read John 13:1–17 together as the Holy Spirit leads and pray together. Other than that, just enjoy the experience and keep things lighthearted!

(If your husband is going through his 31-Day Pursuit Challenge, you'll be going through the same pursuit today. Serve each other!)

___ *Check here when you've completed this pursuit.*

FIELD NOTES

Thoughts, feelings, or observations about today's pursuit?

14

Freedom in Honesty

*Therefore, confess your sins to one another and pray for one
another, that you may be healed. The prayer of a righteous
person has great power as it is working.*

JAMES 5:16

Honesty isn't easy. I suppose it would be if you were perfect and
had nothing ugly to share, but sadly (and despite my best efforts)
that's not the case for me.

One area where I struggle with being honest is in my spending.
Small discretionary purchases catch up to me. Twenty dollars
here, fifteen dollars there. . . it all adds up. The problem is that
it adds up whether or not I consciously add it up. Suddenly, I've
spent hundreds of dollars that weren't in our monthly budget. In
the past, I've hidden overspending from my husband because I
was ashamed and afraid of how he'd react. I won't explicitly lie,
but I'll share half-truths or just avoid sharing my mistake. I tend

to want to hide, when the exact opposite is what I need and our marriage needs most. It's only through honesty with ourselves and each other that we can grow, be sanctified, and in turn, be strengthened as a couple. We need *more* transparency for a healthy marriage, not less! Intentional transparency is difficult, but it's the only way. Honesty usually marks the trailhead to the path of life—it's the beginning of repentance and the start of sanctification.

For those in the Christian faith, human imperfection is where the good news of the gospel begins. Acknowledging and confessing our own sin is the first step toward reconciliation with God. When we see our sin for what it truly is—willful rebellion from our powerful, holy God—we see clearly how gravely we fall short of righteousness.

But though our sin marks the beginning of the gospel, it's certainly not its end! Our imperfection exposes our raw need for a Savior—a need God miraculously met in Christ on the cross. "But God shows his love for us in that while we were still sinners, Christ died for us" (Romans 5:8). Perhaps the most compelling truth of the gospel is that you are fully exposed to a perfect and holy God and still—*still*—you are completely loved.

But God doesn't just give us salvation and end the story there. He lovingly sanctifies us in this life, making us holy until the day we die. Timothy Keller once tweeted, "God invites us to come as we are, not to stay as we are." Why else does James, in today's Scripture verse, instruct believers to confess their sins to each other? Honesty about sin (confessing it) serves at least two purposes: to reconcile relationships and to sanctify your heart.

Marriage offers an unparalleled arena for honesty, transparency, and therefore, love between two imperfect people. The struggles I face in our marriage, like selfishness (not wanting to give any more of myself than is required), ungratefulness (complaining), and guilt (mommy guilt, me-not-doing-or-being-enough guilt), enslave me until I confess them first to God, then to my husband. Lasting freedom only begins when I stop fighting alone. Namely, when I ask my husband for help and start living with full, unfiltered transparency. Our motto for our marriage and in our family life is, "Lights on, windows and doors wide open."

Confession of our sins to each other has become a constant rhythm for us. I've given him permission to ask me anything, and in return I've promised him (and myself) that I'll never lie, no matter how hard the truth is. I'll often schedule times to talk with him to divulge areas where the Holy Spirit is convicting me. I'll say something like, "Can we talk later tonight? I have something I need to share with you." When the time comes, we're both more ready for an intentional conversation, where emotions are less of a factor and we can both prepare our hearts in advance through prayer.

One remarkable outcome of my transparency is that it makes my husband want to be more transparent with me. Mutual repentance isn't always easy, but God is faithful to use us both in his sanctifying work in our individual hearts. As a result, our marriage flourishes as our understanding of the gospel deepens.

In turn, our love for each other grows as our affections for Jesus are stirred and amplified.

As a wife, you can pursue, encourage, and support your husband by confessing your own sin with full confidence in Christ. He knows you're not perfect! There's no need to pretend otherwise. Pursue your husband by living transparently; there is too much at stake in life and marriage to let sin linger unconfessed. Not only that, but the rewards of living honestly with your husband are unsurpassed.

NOTE

God's grace covers sin for salvation, but the earthly consequences of sin still remain. For example, if you've been hiding something for a long time and suddenly share it, he may be hurt or angry. That isn't to say that you can't work through anything with Jesus, but it will likely take time to rebuild trust and reconcile your relationship. Knowing that, use wisdom in how and when you confess sin, but don't delay. While the reconciliation process might look daunting, the alternative is much, much worse. If necessary, seek help (pastoral care, counseling) in reconciling your relationship.

On the flip side, you can further pursue your husband by extending forgiveness to him when he confesses sin to you.

REFLECT

Have you ever hidden, covered, or masked the truth in your marriage? If so, what were you hiding?

Have there been times in your marriage when honesty has been a big relief? If so, when? Why?

PRAY

Ask God for sensitivity and strength for you and your husband as you work on transparency with each other. Thank God for his continued guidance on this path of honesty.

Pursuit 14

ACT   ◉◉◎ ⏐ $ $ $

First, take some time and pray. Ask the Holy Spirit to reveal areas in your heart that need to be surrendered and confessed to God. Just sit and listen for a few minutes. Reflect and write down whatever comes to mind.

Make a date with your husband to share what you have learned (good, bad, or otherwise). Preface your conversation by explaining why you value transparency with him and want to pursue him by being completely honest in full light of the gospel.

___ *Check here when you've completed this pursuit.*

FIELD NOTES

Thoughts, feelings, or observations about today's pursuit?

DAY

15

Proactive Kindness

*When the goodness and loving kindness of God our Savior
appeared, he saved us, not because of works done by us in
righteousness, but according to his own mercy, by the washing of
regeneration and renewal of the Holy Spirit, whom he poured
out on us richly through Jesus Christ our Savior.*

TITUS 3:4–6

One evening when our first daughter was younger, Ryan and I
were sitting on the couch together. He was watching a movie
and I was nursing the baby while flipping through a parent-
ing "how-to" book. Out of nowhere, he looked over at me and
said, "You're an incredible wife and mother." He lovingly and so
sweetly told me, "I see all you do, and I want you to know how
much I appreciate it." Still reading, I glanced up at him and said,
"Don't play with your beard, it's annoying."

To this day, I have no idea what I was thinking! Talk about
poor timing. I heard and appreciated the kind words he said

to me, but I was more concerned about communicating what I wanted to say rather than responding to what he said. My lack of tact sounds funny now, but it definitely wasn't at the time. My unkind words left him feeling hurt, frustrated, and unloved.

We talked, I apologized, and he extended grace my way. Over the years, God has shown us exactly how our moments of impatience and unkindness toward each other affect our marriage. If we're not careful, our terse tones and exacting, ungraceful language wears us down. It shortens our patience and stifles our mutual joy. In short, our marriage without kindness is a marriage void of intentional love.

The reverse is also true: when we're mutually kind to each other, it multiplies the amount of joy and love in our marriage. That's because kindness is love in action. The above verse from Titus says, "When the goodness and loving kindness of God our Savior appeared, he saved us." Catch that? *Loving kindness.* It was because of his love and through kindness that God saved us. In Christ, we are the eternal recipients of God's tangible action of love on the cross—or, his *kindness.*

In 1 Corinthians 13:4–5, Paul states, "Love is patient and kind . . . it is not arrogant or rude." In Galatians, he connects kindness and love as fruits of the Spirit (5:22–23), The two are inextricable. Love without kindness is untrue love. Ryan and I often speak of kindness as love with its sleeves rolled up—it's the work of love. Kindness is love that isn't afraid to get its hands dirty. It actively engages in the tasks of love by going out of its way to serve others, give freely, and acknowledge genuine affection.

Jesus is God's loving kindness toward us. He came to earth and wasn't afraid to get his hands dirty. How many times did he engage in tasks of love through serving others during his ministry? He freely gave his life as a means of redemption for God's chosen. Not because of anything we have done, "but according to his own mercy" (Titus 3:5).

God is love (1 John 4:8), and he embodies the type of love that isn't afraid to get involved. God's sovereign pull—his drawing you near through Jesus—is the kindest, most active display of love imaginable. Friend, you have been pursued and found by God himself. You have received the most vivid, tangible, and unprecedented act of kindness in the history of everything!

As a wife, I desperately need to be reminded of this truth. I must cling to it daily. It's easy to default to being unintentionally unkind to our husbands. I know that's the case for me. If I'm not careful, I can speak in ways that are sharp, insensitive, and self-focused. I can be thoughtless and unaware of opportunities to appreciate and acknowledge him. But, armed with the experience of God's kindness in Christ, I can learn to love my husband more kindly.

Remember how God pursued you, his kindness, and the lengths he went to in order to bring you back to him. Then, out of his loving and kind pursuit of you, pursue your husband.

REFLECT

What are some ways you've been kind to your husband in the past and it's made a big impression?

List three tangible ways you can consistently show your husband love through kindness.

PRAY

Ask God for help showing your husband love through acts of kindness. Pray for self-awareness in this area.

Pursuit 15

ACT

⊙⊙⊙ | $ $ $

Go out of your way to show your husband kindness today. You could serve him, encourage him, give him a small gift, bring him lunch, or do whatever else comes to mind. Put your hands to the work of love by showing him proactive kindness.

___ *Check here when you've completed this pursuit.*

FIELD NOTES

Thoughts, feelings, or observations about today's pursuit?

HEADS-UP!

You're just about halfway through the 31-Day Pursuit Challenge. Keep up the great work! As a reminder, the last day is designed as a finale, and for that reason, it's a big one. Have you looked at the final day yet? Remember, if your husband is going through the challenge too, you can plan Day 31 together.

As a wife, I choose
to honor my husband,
not because I am weak,
but because I am strong.

DAY

16

Insistent Selflessness

Love is patient and kind; love does not envy or boast; it is not arrogant or rude. It does not insist on its own way; it is not irritable or resentful; it does not rejoice at wrongdoing, but rejoices with the truth.

1 CORINTHIANS 13:4–6

Ryan is in a guys' leadership group at church that meets every other week to talk about life, doctrine, and stirring their affections for Christ. He's not a pastor, but he got invited to attend a pastors' conference in Reno, Nevada (of all places, I know). The trip was slated to last three days and two nights, and the event took place midweek. It was time away that I was reluctant to give, but I knew he would get a lot out of it, so I agreed. Once we were on the same page, I mentally geared myself up to take care of our two young kids solo for a few days. I felt confident before Ryan left, but that quickly changed. The first day ended up being a total train wreck.

The moment he was gone, it was as if our three-year-old suddenly lost her ability to hear my voice, let alone obey. It was meltdown after meltdown, topped off with the fact that our other baby girl decided to cut four teeth within the span of about fifteen minutes. She didn't want to be put down—whining and crying all day without any relent or napping (for anyone).

Needless to say, it was one of the worst days we Frederick girls have had to date. When Ryan texted me to check in that evening, he asked how everything was going and told me he was having a great time and learning a ton. My message back was not as cheery: "I'm really glad you're having a great time, but honestly I don't want to hear about it right now because today has literally been the worst day ever."

I couldn't wait for him to get home. Feelings of selfishness stewed in my mind, along with plans for all the justified alone time I would have once he returned. My inner dialogue raged with frustration as I let feelings of discontentment creep in. I imagined Ryan being stuck at home in my shoes on that awful day and how my sinful heart would relish in his pretend agony. Ugh. I cringe when I think of how angry I was that first day he was gone. I wince when I recall how quickly I forgot that Jesus' presence never left me—and that despite the storm of that day, I could have had peace. But still, God was graciously present with me in that ugly moment though I had completely lost sight of how he pursued me first and why.

Today's passage came to mind: "[Love] is not irritable or resentful." While my frustration may have been justified, my resentment wasn't. I had let "insisting on my own way" (v. 5) creep in and steal my love for Ryan—my desire for his best in that circumstance.

As I was frustrated in my selfishness those three days, God pursued me. The Holy Spirit used Romans 5:8 to remind me how "God shows his love for us in that while we were still sinners, Christ died for us." He lovingly reminded me of Jesus' complete selflessness on the cross. How Christ was mocked, tortured, and separated from his Father, yet he never became resentful. He was powerful enough to abandon his mission, yet he never insisted on his own way. Through reminding me of his relentless love, God transformed and taught me to love my husband. In that week, it was Christ's love that helped me give the gift of time to my husband, despite the craziness I was experiencing in his absence.

Whenever I pursue my husband by giving him time to be refreshed and renewed by Jesus, he comes back filled up in every way. He's more loving, kind, gracious, and ready to give of himself because God has poured out his goodness into him.

Looking back, we probably could have planned ahead a little better for Ryan's time away. We could have enlisted a babysitter or prepared meals in advance. Live and learn, right? In this case, I'm so grateful we lived—and one tangible thing I learned from it all is that as fierce wives, we can radically bless our husbands by allowing them time to encounter God.

REFLECT

Have there been times when you or your husband have come back changed or refreshed from an experience? If so, how did that affect your relationship?

Do you actively encourage your husband to spend focused time with God or building gospel-centered friendships? If so, how? If not, how can you start?

PRAY

Ask God to help you identify ways to give each other refreshment, specifically to encounter God.

Pursuit 16

ACT

⊙⊙◔ | $ $ $

Give your husband the gift of time. Give him a "free pass" to spend two hours however he needs it most. No strings attached!

Do whatever you can to graciously alleviate his burdens today or tonight so he can focus on Jesus. Pursue him by giving him the time he needs to seek the face of God.

____ *Check here when you've completed this pursuit.*

FIELD NOTES

Thoughts, feelings, or observations about today's pursuit?

HEADS-UP!

Tomorrow you'll be dreaming and envisioning the future. Make sure both of you have at least thirty minutes set aside.

17

Dreams, Desires, and Delighting in the Lord

Delight yourself in the LORD, and he will give you the desires of your heart. Commit your way to the LORD; trust in him, and he will act.

PSALM 37:4–5

In the early years of our marriage, Ryan and I had big dreams. We wanted a lot from life and felt fairly well equipped to go get it. Tragically, we often focused on God's *gifts* more than we worshipped him as the *giver*. About six years into our marriage, we moved twelve hundred miles away from home to Southern California. We thought we were calling the shots, but God was actively calling us away from all we knew, and in the process, he was doing a miracle. He began uprooting all of our misplaced desires and selfish ambitions. He opened our eyes to our subtle idolatry and graciously surrounded us with people and friends who valued God's Word in ways we had never experienced. He showed us that he is the only one worth desiring and the only reason to dream. It wasn't an easy journey, and we were confronted with many difficult, faith-building seasons. In the end, I'm eternally grateful to God because in each case we were always forced to place our trust in him. And he, of course, showed himself faithful every single time.

When you read today's verse, what comes to mind? What does it mean to "delight yourself in the Lord"? How exactly will he "give you the desires of your heart"? The first part is more intuitive: delighting in the Lord simply means loving him more than anyone or anything. The second question isn't as easy to answer, but let's try.

When we delight ourselves in God, he occupies his correct place in our lives as King, Savior, and Provider. Absolutely nothing matters more than he does, and when that's the case, we only want what God wants. His sovereign desires overtake our fleshly desires—they're instilled deep in our hearts and radiate outward into tangible action. God's act of giving us the desires of our hearts involves him graciously *redefining* what we care about as he transforms our hearts from the inside out. Then, as our will aligns with his will, our desires are fulfilled.

Now, you may have had this understanding all along, but it was groundbreaking for our twentysomething hearts! We realized that gospel-centered desire and ambition are good, but they will never trump our highest call, which is to desire God most.

Pursuing the dreams and desires God has placed in your hearts as a married couple can be a beautiful journey of learning how to trust God. When we rest in the knowledge that he is more than able to do far more than we ask or think (Ephesians 3:20), our vision is big but our burden is light. He will never disappoint. We need only stay the course and walk and live securely in him, all the while trusting in *his* divine plan more than our own.

Why all this background about godly desires? Because today's pursuit is all about desiring and dreaming about the things God has placed in your hearts. Maybe it's been a while since you and your husband went to God and prayed to know his desires for your marriage. Or maybe neither of you have ever really put a lot of thought into it. I would encourage you to go to the Bible and read about how God's people learned to trust him and to hold onto the promises he gave them.

Day-to-day life doesn't readily offer opportunities to discuss God's vision and purpose for your marriage. And sometimes life's demands (a mortgage payment, job security, general busyness) can choke the faith out of daily living. Today's challenge is to have a conversation with your husband about God's vision for your lives. Specifically, how is God calling *him* to step out in faith and trust God more? One of the most loving things you can do for your husband is to urge him toward a more radical faith in Jesus. It's time to explore your husband's God-given talents, dreams, and goals—and look for ways to support him in faithfully pursuing them for God's ultimate glory.

REFLECT

When you were a newlywed, how did you view things like vision? Dreams? Goals? Talents? How have your views evolved or changed since then?

Have you and your husband clearly articulated your vision for your marriage? If so, what is it?

PRAY

Praise God for the dreams and goals he has put in the heart of your husband. Ask God for insight and wisdom in further defining your husband's purpose and dreams.

Pursuit 17

ACT

⊙⊙⊙ | $ $ $

Spend at least thirty minutes tonight discussing your husband's purpose and dreams. Ask him what he's passionate about and how he feels called to serve Jesus. Explore ways that you can come alongside him through prayer, actions, and encouragement. Whatever you discuss, write it down! If possible, create a tangible plan to begin stepping out in faith as the Holy Spirit prompts.

___ *Check here when you've completed this pursuit.*

(If your husband is doing the 31-Day Pursuit Challenge, you might recall doing this exercise yourself five days ago. It's his turn!)

FIELD NOTES

Thoughts, feelings, or observations about today's pursuit?

HEADS-UP!

In two days, you'll be preparing a special at-home meal. You may want to begin planning!

18

Thoughtful Creation

O Lord, how manifold are your works! In wisdom have you made them all; the earth is full of your creatures. Here is the sea, great and wide, which teems with creatures innumerable, living things both small and great. There go the ships, and Leviathan, which you formed to play in it.

PSALM 104:24–26

One of my favorite gifts I've ever received from Ryan came while we were dating in high school. He bought me a charm bracelet for our one-year dating anniversary. That year had been full of incredible memories, funny jokes and circumstances, and unique milestones in our relationship, all of which he wanted me to remember. Each charm, of course, represented one of those memories. Best. Gift. Ever! Young, sixteen-year-old Selena was giddy (I still am), and I wore that bracelet proudly every day. All these years later that little charm bracelet still makes my heart skip a beat and puts a goofy smile on my face. All the feelings and memories rush back, and my heart feels full.

What made his gift so great? It wasn't the item itself; it was its thoughtfulness and what the gift represented. He took the time to pursue me by considering what would speak to my heart. At sixteen years of age, it's easy for us to keep our special someone on the front of our minds (at least for us girls, am I right?). But as time goes on and marriage becomes more familiar, life happens, new routines and rhythms begin to take over, and it's easy to forget the importance of intentional thoughtfulness.

Today's verse reminds us that God's intentionality and thoughtfulness are vast and eternal. "In wisdom," he made all his works! Everything we see is the result of his loving, meticulous care and craftsmanship. Every aspect of this earth declares his glory. He created "living things both small and great."

Have you ever stopped to admire a single flower? The biological systems it took for that flower to bloom are nothing short of miraculous. He could have given us a drab world to occupy, but he didn't. We have enough evidence in our backyards to marvel at his power, creativity, and sovereignty for the rest of our lives!

Now, take a moment to consider how intricately you've been created. Every atom, cell, blood vessel, thought, and emotion. How about your husband? It's impossible to think we have been created and captivated by a God who was thoughtless or unintentional.

Every facet of creation bears the mark of his craftsmanship. His thoughtfulness is undeniable. Now consider this: you were not only created by God, but you were made in his image (Genesis

1:27), and as his image bearer, you have the ability to think and act creatively! In other words, you can be extraordinarily thoughtful. That's where today's challenge comes in.

What would your marriage be like if you applied a fraction of your full, God-given ability to thoughtfulness in how you pursue your husband? What if you viewed your relationship as something you were beautifully and carefully crafting with God's help?

If you're reading this and feeling a stirring in your soul, God is at work. He may be challenging you to love more selflessly—more thoughtfully. If so, embrace the challenge!

The thing about thoughtfulness is that there are no shortcuts or substitutes. You can't buy it and you can't fake it. Thoughtfulness can only be handcrafted, by you, with meticulous care. . . which is perhaps why it's one of the most valuable ways you can pursue your husband.

REFLECT

How has your husband's thoughtfulness in the past made you feel?

How have you been thoughtful toward your husband in the past? What are a few tangible ways you can be intentionally thoughtful toward him in the future?

PRAY

Thank God for his thoughtful, beautiful, and intentional creation! Maybe even list out a few of your favorite parts. Ask the Holy Spirit to lead you in how to create and cultivate thoughtfulness in your relationship with your husband.

Pursuit 18

ACT

⏱ ⏱ ⏱ | $ $ $

Do something thoughtful for your husband. It could be breakfast in bed, a small gesture, a short meaningful text, or an act of service. The only requirement is that you go out of your way to do something that makes your man feel loved and pursued.

___ *Check here when you've completed this pursuit.*

FIELD NOTES

Thoughts, feelings, or observations about today's pursuit?

HEADS-UP!

Tomorrow you'll be doing some writing . . . romantic writing. Make sure to carve out a little extra time!

A marriage without friendship is like a bird without wings.

DARLENE SCHACHT

19

The Articulate Romantic

My beloved is radiant and ruddy,
distinguished among ten thousand.

SONG OF SOLOMON 5:10

What is it about love songs that makes them so compelling? Music has an intrinsic ability to affect human emotion, but that can't be the only reason romantic music is so special. Love songs (good ones, that is) continue to captivate human hearts because for many of us, they effectively put to words the ideas we wish we could articulate. Many times, couples identify "their song" because something about it just seems to capture and communicate how they feel about each other. The same could be said about any type of creative writing: poetry, music, or prose. Something about the written word uniquely affects our hearts and minds.

Solomon, a king known for his wisdom, understood the power of artistic expression impeccably. The above passage comes from a section of Song of Solomon titled, "The Bride Praises Her Beloved." The entire book is a collection of love poetry that follows the romantic exchanges between a husband and wife. It's truly a beautiful representation of love in pursuit, but also of the power of creative writing for the *purpose* of pursuit.

A few days back, I mentioned the notes that Ryan and I gave to each other between classes. To this day I still have most of them. Every once in a while I'll crack open our memory box and reminisce. It's funny (and heartwarming) to see how our feelings progressed from the early notes to the later ones. I'm so happy we wrote them, and I'm equally glad I managed to keep them.

I've always been (and forever will be) a fan of handwritten anything: essays, recipes, letters, etc. Writing something by hand is personal, intimate, and even revealing, as many scholars will tell you. Reading something written by hand is one of my favorite things to do. I feel as if the writer is speaking to me, but I can feel and experience their words in the safety of the letter. I don't have to worry about my reaction—I can simply read and absorb.

For today's pursuit, you're tasked with writing something romantic to your husband that communicates your love and desire for him. The details are up to you. The only catch is your project must be physical (no social media posts), and it has to include written words of love to him.

Today's pursuit may challenge you to step out of your comfort zone. If that's the case, I encourage you to face it head-on! Communicating romantically can be intimidating; especially when doing so creatively. You may even discount your ability to express yourself romantically because you don't consider yourself gifted. Or maybe it's just been a long time since you've used language like this with your husband. It's okay! You don't need to impress anyone, just be authentic and honest. He's sure to feel loved by whatever you create and however you articulate.

REFLECT

Think about a time when an artistic expression (a book, song, poem, painting, etc.) really moved you. How did it make you feel, and why?

PRAY

Ask God for refreshed creativity and bravery to express your love to your husband.

Pursuit 19

ACT

Pursue your husband by putting pen to paper. Write a poem, song, short story, or letter that expresses your love and gratefulness for him. If it doesn't come easy for you, keep trying! It's good to labor over romance. The objective isn't perfection; it's authenticity.

When you're finished, read your words aloud or present them to your husband in a note—do whatever feels most natural, but make sure to stretch yourself!

(If your husband is going through his own 31-Day Pursuit Challenge, he did this two days ago. Your turn! You didn't think you were off the hook, did you?)

____ *Check here when you've completed this pursuit.*

FIELD NOTES

Thoughts, feelings, or observations about today's pursuit?

DAY
20

Unceasing
Celebration

*Day by day, attending the temple together and breaking bread
in their homes, they received their food with glad and generous
hearts, praising God and having favor with all the people.*

ACTS 2:46–47

Jesus' pursuit of our hearts spans from the garden to the cross
and beyond. Every covenant God made with Israel points to his
ultimate mission of reconciling his beloved people back to him.
Each one, pointing to a Savior yet to come, and foreshadowing
relational wholeness between God and humanity. Acts shows us
the aftermath of Christ's resurrection as fulfillment of those early
covenants. What it must have been like to be alive in those days!
To feel so nearly and tangibly the outpouring of grace . . . talk
about a celebration!

In the book of Acts we see the beginning of the early church.
We get front-row seats to the first stages of the world-changing

culture shock that started after Jesus ascended into heaven. The entire world was turned on its head as the news of Christ rang through the streets and towns: "Finally, Jesus satisfied the requirements of the old covenant! Jew and Gentile are justified by faith in Christ!" The impact of such a transition can't be overstated. These men and women, who had lived their entire lives as slaves under the law, were suddenly and absolutely free because of a man named Jesus Christ. Can you imagine their joy and relief? Can you picture how they must have celebrated?

Today's Scripture passage provides a peek into exactly *how* the early church celebrated the gospel: By "attending the temple together and breaking bread in their homes," and by receiving their food with "glad and generous hearts, praising God and having favor with all the people." In other words, they gathered as a community of believers, dined together, and praised God with glad, generous, and grateful hearts.

As fellow believers, you and I can also participate in the celebration; it's our faith tradition too! Though we may not fully understand how the early Christians felt, we can experience radical freedom in Christ as sinners once lost, now saved by grace. He has taken our debt, paid it in full, and adopted us as daughters of the King. Friend, we have cause to celebrate! We, too, have reason to live with extraordinary joy.

Those in the early church were profoundly happy—not because of their circumstances (since they were under constant persecution)—but because of their newfound life and freedom in Christ. Profound, ceaseless joy is always the case for believers.

For children of God, every church gathering holds new meaning, every meal tastes richer, and every relationship now bears the mark of the gospel—*especially* marriage.

In marriage, your feelings of love and desire to show it may shift constantly depending on countless factors: your blood sugar, how much sleep you've had, whether or not you're in an argument, and any mixture of other things. However (and that's a *big* however), your source of life and freedom never changes. Your reason for celebration is more constant than the rising sun! He never changes, but we do—our hearts forget the weight of what Jesus did.

The key to lifelong celebration is stirring our hearts for Jesus, recalling the weight of our sin, and most importantly, remembering that God saved our needy souls. As long as we remember the gospel, we remember to celebrate.

If you and your husband are both believers, you can marvel in and celebrate Christ together—especially when you break bread. Every meal can serve a higher purpose of celebration if you're intentional about them. Grateful hearts often begin at the dinner table and radiate outward into every other facet of life.

Fierce sister, I pray that your household is filled with joy and celebration because of Jesus. When you break bread with your husband, I hope it's with glad, generous, and grateful hearts. As you do, you'll be walking in the same joy experienced by your brothers and sisters in Christ thousands of years ago.

REFLECT

What was one of the best meals you've shared in the past? What made it special?

Would you say your life is marked by celebration in Christ? Why or why not? How can you improve?

PRAY

Thank God for his ceaseless gift of salvation in Christ. Ask him for increased joy and gratefulness during every meal as a family.

Pursuit 20

ACT

⊙ ⊙ ⊙ | $ $ $

Plan an at-home date night (or picnic, depending on the time of year). Create a meal plan and prepare an extravagant display of celebration and affection. Consider cooking him a special meal. Light some candles and set the atmosphere; maybe even dress nicer than usual, and definitely eliminate distractions (phones put away).

As you share your meal, celebrate your relationship; celebrate your husband. Give thanks to God and reflect on all that he's done for you and in your marriage. You may want to let your husband know what to expect in advance so he can prepare accordingly (by wearing appropriate attire or moving things around in his schedule).

___ *Check here when you've completed this pursuit.*

FIELD NOTES

Thoughts, feelings, or observations about today's pursuit?

DAY
21

A Prayerful Pursuit

Let us then with confidence draw near to the throne of grace, that
we may receive mercy and find grace to help in time of need.

Hebrews 4:16

Prayer is a beautiful, wonderful, and sacrificial privilege. It's a gift and a blessing. Before I met Ryan, I was praying for him. And now that we've been married for a while, I'm praying for him more than ever.

There's just something intimate and soul-bonding about praying for your husband. Only you know some of the battles that he's facing: What's he dealing with at work? What areas is he working to grow in? How are his family relationships? How's his passion for Jesus?

It's easy to complain and make excuses for not praying diligently, but we must fiercely fight for our marriages by contending for our husbands in prayer. A praying woman is a woman that recognizes her need for Jesus. For me, a lacking prayer life is an obvious indication that I'm steeped in self-reliance. Prayer should be our first and most powerful weapon against any division within or opposition against our marriages.

As the author of Hebrews wrote in today's verse, "Let us then with confidence draw near to the throne of grace." As we discovered yesterday, grace wasn't always normal, but the cross changed everything. Because of Jesus, we can now approach the very *throne of God*—even more than that, we're always welcome! When we pray, we're like thirsty children in our parents' bedroom, asking for a drink of water. Except our heavenly Father never wakes up tired and grumpy.

God lovingly reminds me to pray for Ryan with intentional persistence. Here's a list of prayers I keep handy for when I feel stuck. Each one starts, "I pray . . ." (Write your husband's name in the blanks):

- For _____'s relationship with God.

- That _____ would have a soft heart toward God.

- For God's blessing over _____.

- For _____ to be a devoted spiritual leader of our family.

- For _____ to have a heart for our children.

- For _____ to have wisdom and discernment.

- For _____'s emotional, mental, and physical health.

- For _____ to flourish in his work.

- For _____'s strength to resist sexual temptation.

Many times I'll also pray for myself as it pertains to my husband: *God, help me have a soft, tender heart toward Ryan. Help me respect him and love him in ways that speak to him.* It's amazing how richly and obviously we can see God work in our marriage when we consistently turn to him in prayer.

Remember, fierce wife, the power of your prayers! When you pray, you are conversing with the Designer of marriage itself—the King of the universe and the eternal Savior who relentlessly contends for you, your husband, *and* your marriage.

REFLECT

How have you seen God work in your marriage through prayer?

How can you pray more intentionally for your husband from this moment forward?

PRAY

Ask God to open your eyes to your need for prayer. Pray for a deeper, richer, and more consistent prayer life.

ACT

Today's challenge has two parts. The first part is to pray for your husband through the sample list provided. Write your prayers down and create a reminder to revisit them in a few months to see how God is working.

The second part of today's challenge is to pray for your husband before going to bed. Ask him what's on his heart before offering to pray for him. Make sure to hold hands as a symbol of unity and agreement.

___ *Check here when you've completed this pursuit.*

FIELD NOTES

Thoughts, feelings, or observations about today's pursuit?

HEADS-UP!

On Day 24, you'll be remaking your first, or favorite, date. Start thinking about what that might entail!

DAY

22

The Gift of Gladness

Therefore welcome one another as Christ has welcomed you,
for the glory of God.

ROMANS 15:7

By the time I wake up, Ryan is usually gone to the gym. I don't mind that he's not there—I love my morning routine. I love my kids so much, but I love them so much *better* if I can have just a little bit of quiet time before the circus opens for the day. If I can manage to sneak in enough time before the kids wake up, I have the perfect sequence of activities that set my day down a much more pleasant path.

On an ideal morning I'll get up, pour some coffee, grab my Bible and a journal, and spend some one-on-one time with Jesus. Then, if I have a few extra minutes, I like to read one of the four or five books I'm working through (that's not to sound impressive, my reading list tends to be a scattered, hot mess). Usually a few pages in, one or both of the kids will join me in the living room, and we're off to the races.

It's right about then that Ryan returns from working out. He's typically sweaty, tired, and ready for some coffee of his own. I know when he's home because I can see him pull into the driveway just before hearing his familiar key jingling as he unlocks the front door. It's at that exact moment that, no matter what has happened up to that point, I have a choice to make: How will I greet my husband for the first time that day?

Here's the thing: I'm a verbal processor. Many mornings, I've been processing things *in my head* all night, and I can't wait to, well, verbalize them. Even more than that, I can't wait to verbalize them to my husband! My eagerness—sometimes cheery, sometimes grumpy—is where I can get myself into trouble.

You see, Ryan isn't a verbal processor. He's a nonverbal processor. If I start talking to him at full speed the second the door opens . . . well, let's just say it's not his favorite thing.

Or even worse, if I'm in a grumpy mood for whatever reason (pick one: up all night with the baby, not feeling well, stressed out because we're having guests over, etc.), and I inundate him immediately, it never goes well. In those cases, his first greeting from me, *his wife*, is a brash, hurried, frustration-filled barrage of word vomit.

Thankfully, Ryan recently sat me down and explained to me how this makes him feel. He hates it. As it turns out, all he really wants from me first is a "Good morning" and a kiss. "After that," he said, "everything else is fair game."

Message received! Deal.

Believe it or not, the underlying issue in our scenario had to do with courtesy, mutual respect, and genuine gladness (or the lack thereof). While I was certainly glad to see my husband, I wasn't showing him. For him, those mornings where I'd start talking immediately felt like a slap in the face. We hadn't even greeted each other yet—how could I dive right into the business of the day?

Today's passage from the book of Romans changed my entire perspective on how I greet my husband with gladness. Paul's simple, profound words, "Welcome one another as Christ has welcomed you," continue to convict me. Was I being intentionally rude to Ryan by not greeting him in the morning before off-loading my mental cargo? If I was grumpy, probably. Most of the time I wasn't being rude on purpose. However, I *was* being selfish, and Christ would never welcome me with selfishness. Quite the opposite! Christ welcomes me with love, warmth, strength, and gladness. He diligently looks for his lost sheep, and once he finds them, he rejoices (Luke 15:5)!

In the case of our morning greetings, Ryan wasn't refusing to talk. He actually *did* want to hear what I had to say. He just felt steamrolled. I've since realized that, as his wife, I have a unique opportunity every morning (or whenever we're reunited) to greet my husband with gladness, welcoming him into my life "as Christ has welcomed me."

If you've been married for a while, you understand that it's not always perfect mornings and ideal circumstances. There will be times when glad communication feels excruciatingly difficult—even fake. I assure you, you're not being fake by taking care in how you greet your husband.

Also, I get it, sometimes it's easier to be selfish in how you act toward your husband—*especially* when you feel like venting. After all, he's stuck with you, right? How else will he understand how you feel? He'll get over it. While that's true (and your covenant is cause for celebration), that attitude flies in the face of gospel-fueled gladness. Is your husband fragile? Probably not. Ryan isn't. I just know he feels a whole lot stronger, uplifted, and encouraged when I intentionally greet him with gladness in the form of a kind word and a sweet kiss.

After all, today's challenge isn't about our right as wives to express how we're feeling. That's a separate conversation. Today is about our heart orientation toward our husbands and our willingness to pursue and love them by "welcoming them" as Christ has welcomed us, "for the glory of God" (Romans 15:7).

Fierce wife, greet your husband with all the genuine gladness and joy warranted you through the gospel. Pursue him with fresh eyes each day and greet him with gladness every chance you get. Even the smallest gestures of gospel-fueled love will have a profound impact on your marriage.

REFLECT

As a wife, what practical reasons do you have for welcoming your husband "as Christ has welcomed you"?

How can you be more intentional in how you greet your husband with gladness?

PRAY

Thank God for the loving moments you've shared with your husband. Ask the Holy Spirit for renewed gladness toward him.

Pursuit 22

ACT

🕐 🕑 🕒 | $ $ $

Today's challenge isn't as much a one-time thing as it is the beginning of a new habit (or refreshing an old one). The next time you see your husband, greet him with genuine, glad affection. You decide what that means to you. Just be sure to welcome him! It could be a kiss, a hug, a smile, or affectionate words. If you feel led, discuss how you can work on pursuing each other more intentionally through greetings.

___ *Check here when you've completed this pursuit.*

FIELD NOTES

Thoughts, feelings, or observations about today's pursuit?

DAY

23

Untiring Love

I am sure that neither death nor life, nor angels nor rulers, nor things present nor things to come, nor powers, nor height nor depth, nor anything else in all creation, will be able to separate us from the love of God in Christ Jesus our Lord.

ROMANS 8:38–39

One of my all-time favorite authors is Louisa May Alcott. I cherish her book *Little Women*, and, having two young daughters, I pretty much cry every time I read it. In one special moment between Marmee (the mother) and Jo (the hot-tempered, wild, passionate daughter), Marmee is completely vulnerable and transparent with her daughter Jo.

Jo cries to Marmee, admitting her frustration with her internal struggle with anger and a hot temper. And Marmee, in her tender and guiding way, explains how she herself dealt with intense feelings of rage and anger when she was young like Jo. This comes as a surprise to Jo (and the reader) because the character of Marmee is steadfast, strong, unwavering, peaceful, and overflowing with love for her daughters and duty to her country. The last thing you could imagine Marmee being is angry. In her transparency about her own struggles, she helps Jo understand the depth of love God has for her despite her struggles. Alcott writes, in Marmee's voice,

> *His love and care never tire or change, can never be taken from you, but may become the source of lifelong peace, happiness, and strength. Believe this heartily, and go to God with all your little cares, and hopes, and sins, and sorrows, as freely and confidently as you come to your mother.*[1]

I love how this passage tenderly illustrates the authentic love of Christ. Only because of Jesus can we go to God with all of our concerns and struggles, and he doesn't think any less of us, nor does he grow tired of us! Remember, friends—he knows us more thoroughly than we know ourselves, and he loves us more completely and fully than anyone ever could or will. As we read in today's Scripture passage, *not even death*—spiritual or physical— can separate us from the love of God! Indeed, there is no greater act of love or promise of pursuit than that which we receive in Christ.

Today's pursuit challenge is all about realizing and living out of this message of God's eternal truth and patience. Though God knows us best, good and bad, he loves us most. In the same manner, you know your husband in ways that no one else does. And as a wife you are called to love and respect him, which can be challenging the more you get to know him. That's why marriage is the covenant it is. God designed it as a venue for us to experience authentic grace and true forgiveness—and, fierce wife, it is good!

Trust that when you choose to patiently extend grace to your husband, you are putting the gospel high on display. As you open yourself to loving your husband despite his weaknesses and accepting his love despite your own, go to God's Word and rest in his promises. Remember who you are because of Jesus: fully known, completely loved, accepted, forgiven, and joyfully embraced.

REFLECT

How have you been loved through weakness in the past, by people besides your husband? How did it make you feel?

PRAY

Praise and thank God for his great love for you. Ask him for grace and honesty as you reveal tender spots about each other.

ACT

⏱ ⏱ ⏱ | $ $ $

Write down three ways your husband has shown you love in the midst of sin or weakness. (Example: Once when I was stewing in anger and being unkind to Ryan, he stopped me, hugged me, and asked, "What's wrong, love? How can I help?") Is there a side of you that you often get frustrated with? How does your husband help you with your personal weaknesses?

When you've answered the above questions, share what you've written with your husband. Carve out some time to thank him face-to-face.

___ *Check here when you've completed this pursuit.*

FIELD NOTES

Thoughts, feelings, or observations about today's pursuit?

24

First or Favorite

The steadfast love of the LORD never ceases;
his mercies never come to an end;
they are new every morning;
great is your faithfulness.

LAMENTATIONS 3:22–23

Our first date was full of unforgettable memories, one of which involved Ryan almost getting beat up by a biker in downtown Seattle. Scary, awkward, and hilariously unforgettable.

Ryan had my heart from the very start. We had just had our "Define The Relationship" talk, and I could tell this boy meant business. During our talk he even said, "I wouldn't be thinking about dating you if I didn't think you were someone I could marry someday." It was probably a bit intense for him to say, but he was serious . . . and I didn't mind.

The day after our DTR talk, he left for football camp and I went on a family vacation. We wouldn't see each other for a whole week and would have close to no contact. It felt like the slowest week of my life. By the time we saw each other again, I was beyond excited to hang out with my *new boyfriend.*

We decided to go on an excursion to Seattle—he wanted to take me to one of his favorite parks. I tried to play it cool, but when he pulled into my driveway, my heart skipped a beat. I couldn't wait to spend the whole day together!

Things began pretty uneventfully. We drove thirty miles to Seattle without a problem, except for some reason, the last turn proved difficult. All I remember is that Ryan had his blinker on, preparing to turn left. When there was room for him to turn, he began the turn just fine . . . except he didn't finish it! The engine stalled, and suddenly I was staring into a wall of oncoming traffic. My life flashed before my eyes, I grabbed the handle on my door, and I did everything I could to keep myself from screeching in terror. After all, I didn't want to lose my cool in front of my new boyfriend.

As he scrambled to restart the car, a massive guy on a motorcycle careened toward us. I watched as he slammed on his brakes and squeaked past us just before Ryan restarted the car and bolted out of harm's way. The biker was clearly very angry (and for good reason).

With that, we were out of traffic's way, but we weren't quite in the clear. (My heart beats hard and fast even now when I reminisce about what happened next.) Our angry biker friend sped around the block and intercepted us just a few hundred yards down the road. I still to this day don't know why Ryan pulled over, but Lord bless him, he did. Once we realized that all he wanted was to bash Ryan's face in, Ryan did the brave boyfriend thing and locked all the doors. After enduring a barrage of threats, cuss words, and angry gestures, we drove off.

Minutes later we arrived at the park and found ourselves enthralled in an impromptu, all-out blackberry fight. Like most fun messes in our lives, I started it, and it escalated from there. We both ended up fully submerged in the lake (in our normal clothes) and covered from head to toe in blackberry juice. Afterward, we changed into our still-dry swimsuits and sat on a blanket to talk, have a few snacks, and thank God for letting us survive.

What made that day so unforgettable? Peculiarly enough, it's not almost dying or almost having Ryan's face bashed in. Whenever we think of that day, we immediately remember the blackberries. We remember laughing and having fun—both of us learning what it felt like to be together for the first time. We love recalling all of the feelings of newness, wonder, and nervous excitement. Most of all, being together is what made our first date memorable. Being together makes *life* memorable.

Married life has a way of growing routine. In many ways, it can be the opposite of the first date: filled with daily routines, average moments, and repetitive realities. Routines aren't bad—because real life happens in the in-between moments. Sustainable joy comes from finding contentment and purpose in Christ during life's in-between times.

Following Jesus and marriage share some similarities. The first time you placed your trust in Christ, it was an exhilarating, new experience. But every believer eventually faces dry spells where feelings seem absent and loving God requires diligent devotion.

It's during those times when we must find unshakable joy in the unchanging promises of God. Words like what we read in today's Scripture passage, "His mercies never come to an end; they are new every morning," exist to fill us with fresh hope and stir our affection when we feel dry. In fact, reading those words is almost like recalling a first date experience. We can read, "The steadfast love of the Lord never ceases," and remember the everlasting goodness of God that drew us to him in the first place.

As mentioned in yesterday's pursuit, Jesus never grows tired of loving you. Each promise in Scripture offers a glimpse down memory lane. It's like God is saying, "Don't forget how much I love you, always remember my affection as if it's the first day we met."

Here's how we apply all of this to marriage: God pursues his people because of his covenant promise to do so. In the same way, when you made a covenant promise to your husband, you were promising to pursue him for the rest of your life. Thankfully, with a secure identity in Christ, we have help upholding our end of the marriage promise even when it's difficult.

Do you remember your first date? Do you remember what it felt like to have "new eyes" for each other? Today's challenge is all about recalling your first (or favorite) date as vividly as possible and letting your past history fuel your present pursuit.

REFLECT

Recall a few of your best moments together (not only your first date). Write them down below as a highlight reel of your favorite pieces of relationship history.

Why did the above moments make the list? What made them so special to you?

PRAY

Praise and thank God for giving you your unique history with your husband. Ask God for renewed, fresh eyes to see your husband.

Pursuit 24

ACT

☺☺☺ | ???

Today's challenge is a big one, but you can do it! Do your best to re-create your first or favorite date ever, step by step. If it's just not feasible, get creative: include some things that remind you of your first date (for us, that might be blackberries). Another option is to plan a time and a place where you can meet *as if it's your first date*. Depending on how elaborate you make it, you may want to use today to begin planning a date for the near future. Don't delay! Have fun, be creative, celebrate your history!

(If your husband is going through his own 31-Day Pursuit Challenge on the same schedule, he'll be reading about the same things today. Consider planning together!)

___ *Check here when you've completed this pursuit.*

FIELD NOTES

Thoughts, feelings, or observations about today's pursuit?

DAY

25

Simple, Selfless Affection

[Love] does not insist on its own way.

1 CORINTHIANS 13:5

Today's pursuit is not exclusively about sex or intimacy. If it ends up there, by all means, enjoy the gift God has given you both! However, today's pursuit is about being generous physically toward your husband in small, selfless, and affectionate ways. I know this seems similar to a previous pursuit, and it is (see Day 6). But if you're anything like me, I need reminders on top of reminders about being intentionally affectionate toward my husband. It's not that I'm cold and distant toward him; it's just that life gets busy, and I sometimes forget that his love bucket needs refilling daily.

As wives we can grow weary or tired of physical touch from our husbands because all too often we feel like it *must* lead to sex. This just isn't true. As Ryan has helped me understand (and he assures me this is the case with many of the guys he talks to), men enjoy physical affection even when it's not sexual. Nor does it have to lead *there* every time. According to Ryan, your husband probably agrees.

Even with that, if it does lead to sex, is that a terrible thing? And if things start feeling sexually charged and I'm way too tired to go the distance, can't we talk about it? Of course we can. But for some reason, I'd rather withhold simple gestures of affection for fear of leading him on. As I'm learning, that fear is usually unjustified.

There may be other reasons for forgetting simple affections too. If you're like me, having little children in the house means you're being touched a lot, and at the end of the day, one more hand on your body might make you lose your mind. (Amen?) Or maybe you just aren't a naturally affectionate, touchy-feely person. If that's how you're wired, today's pursuit might require some extra effort, but that's okay. You'll do great! You got this.

Wherever you're at, and whatever level of affection is normal for you, today is your day to show your man plenty of light-hearted physical affection.

First, let's take a quick look at Scripture. In 1 Corinthians 13:4–7, Paul outlines exactly what love is:

> *Love is patient and kind; love does not envy or boast; it is not arrogant or rude. It does not insist on its own way; it is not irritable or resentful; it does not rejoice at wrong-doing, but rejoices with the truth. Love bears all things, believes all things, hopes all things, endures all things.*

The words we're focusing on, "Love does not insist on its own way," can sound like nails on a chalkboard when we actually take them seriously. After all, who *wants* to *not* insist on their own way? I don't. If you're at all like Ryan and me, sometimes your wants are aligned with your husband's and other times, not so much. Things are easy if my husband and I want to go the *same* way, but what if we don't? Who's going to *not insist* on their own way?

The richest marriages are those where both husband and wife consistently choose to give. Instead of taking what they want, they give—by not insisting on their own individual ways. Mutual generosity between spouses has a way of multiplying the richness of the marriage. However, since this is a book specifically for wives, you probably know where this is going . . . (Ryan is letting your husband have it, don't worry.)

Friend, when it comes to giving your husband small, sweet touches of affection, choose to be generous. Choose not to insist on your own way. God's Word instructs us to love radically, and it's not without reason. When we love our husbands God's way—generously, selflessly, kindly, patiently, and so much more—we're actively placing our trust in God. Suddenly our faith has real, tangible evidence, and it's evidence our husbands will see.

So grab your husband's hand, rub his neck, scratch his back, squeeze him tight, and give him a long kiss next time you see him. You are his wife! He longs to feel your touch. Give your husband generous portions of affection and trust that your faith in action will multiply the love you *both* feel in your marriage.

REFLECT

In your own words, what does it mean that "love does not insist on its own way"?

How can you be more affectionate toward your husband in ways that will make him feel most loved?

PRAY

Ask God to lead you in ways that will make your husband feel loved. Pray for help in loving your husband according to God's Word.

Pursuit 25

ACT

⊙⊙⊙ | $ $ $

Show affection to your husband through physical touch, but approach it in a way he will enjoy it most. It could be a simple handhold, a foot rub, or an unexpected back massage.

Be generous in your gestures toward him. Take some time to talk about what kinds of physical touch he enjoys most.

____ *Check here when you've completed this pursuit.*

FIELD NOTES

Thoughts, feelings, or observations about today's pursuit?

HEADS-UP!

Tomorrow you'll be initiating something spontaneous. Make sure you have enough time, but resist the temptation to plan.

DAY

26

Who Cares Where?

For you were called to freedom, brothers.
Only do not use your freedom as an opportunity for the flesh,
but through love serve one another.

GALATIANS 5:13

Overall, Ryan is very much the gas pedal in our life. And yes, I am the brake. He loves to plan and surprise me with spontaneous trips either on the road or across the Atlantic (he once found crazy cheap flights to Munich, so he surprised me with a European backpacking trip out of the blue). We are just as happy and excited to hop in the car and drive to the ocean as we are to hop on a longer flight to a different country. The destination, mode of transportation, and details are never alike, but there is always one thing in common: we're together.

When we were newly married, I prided myself in my ability to be fun, exciting, and spontaneous as a wife. As the years have passed and kids have arrived, spontaneous trips make me panic.

I immediately apply the brakes. My level of willingness to just jump in the car and go isn't what it used to be. That said, I do try to accommodate and even initiate trips, simply because I love my husband and I know it speaks volumes to him. He absolutely loves it whenever I spontaneously announce, "We're packed and the kids are ready! Let's go to the waterfront for a picnic at the beach!"

Spontaneity isn't always convenient, but being willing to initiate it or jump on board when he leads can breathe life into your marriage. That's because spontaneity is pure—it's simple. When you do something spontaneous, the journey is all that matters. Where you go or what you do matters far less than *who* you're going and doing *with*. I know this, but I still find myself pumping the brakes. For me, it comes down to having a willing heart that is ready to jump to action in the name of pursuit.

I love today's verse because it summarizes the core message of Galatians perfectly: "You were called to freedom." Paul continues by saying, "Only do not use your freedom as an opportunity for the flesh, but through love serve one another." The church in Galatia had grown legalistic in response to false doctrine. They had lost their pure faith in Christ. They had slowly stopped believing that Christ's work on the cross was enough, and they'd bought the lie that if they did a few *extra* things (circumcision), they'd be acceptable to God. Friend, there is no path toward freedom or acceptance by God except through the blood of Jesus Christ. He lived the life we couldn't live and died the death we should have died, but why? For freedom. Fierce wife, you are free in Christ!

You're free from fear, anxiety, and worry. You're free from seeking anyone's approval, because you're *already* approved. You're free from having to be in control, because God *is*. And finally, as we read in Galatians, you can use your freedom in Christ to love and serve others—namely, your husband (Galatians 5:13).

This is why spontaneity is good for me—for *you*. Spontaneity is all about freedom. When I'm spontaneous for my husband, it reminds me that I am free to just *let go*. I can rest in Christ, release control, and just see where the wind carries us. Perhaps most importantly (for the purposes of this book), I can show my husband I love him by getting lost *in love* with him.

Every day that you and your husband share is a good gift from a gracious God. Today's challenge is all about embracing that gift. If you trust Jesus, unconditional and abundant joy is yours to have. This is not to say that you will never face trials or hardships (because you will, see John 16:33), but rather that your eternal security—your salvation and redemption—lets you rest easy and enjoy life's simple pleasures in profound ways that are unavailable aside from Christ.

Let spontaneity purify your pursuit. Scrap every agenda but the one that matters: being together. Pursue your man by initiating spontaneous excursions. Whether you're venturing out locally or jet setting around the world, you'll inevitably find yourselves in the exact same place every time: growing closer together, enjoying life in God's grace, and making a few unforgettable memories along the way.

REFLECT

Does spontaneity excite you or scare you? Why?

What is the most spontaneous thing you've ever done?

PRAY

Praise and thank Jesus for freedom. Ask God to release you from fear and worry that would keep you from being spontaneous; ask him for provision for an adventure, and ask for grace in circumstances to make this happen.

Pursuit 26

PLAN

⊙⊙⊙ | $ $ $

Willingly do something spontaneous! Point at a spot on a map and drive, grab ice cream, or just go for a walk. Do something unplanned. If you feel a bit more adventurous, go away for a spontaneous trip. Just get in the car and drive. No hotel reservations, no destination, just each other.

Explain to your husband that *he* is the objective, and it doesn't matter what you do or where you go as long as you're together.

___ *Check here when you've completed this pursuit.*

FIELD NOTES

Thoughts, feelings, or observations about today's pursuit?

27

Worthy Words
and Naked Ninjas

Let no corrupting talk come out of your mouths, but only such
as is good for building up, as fits the occasion, that it may give
grace to those who hear.

EPHESIANS 4:29

I thought I knew how to communicate well. Then I got married.

Ryan and I are typically able to talk to each other or give each other a look and know exactly what the other is thinking. I'm always surprised at how much we say, laugh at, and agree on, all without ever speaking a word. This is one of the main reasons we became friends so quickly, and it's marked our relationship ever since . . . most of the time.

About five years into our marriage, things felt like they were changing for the worse. We had recently purchased our first home and were working on a few projects around the house when an argument erupted. Neither of us remember what we were arguing about, but it was one for the memory books. I remember stomping around the house and throwing laundry (real mature, I know) while "clearly" communicating how wrong he was, or how he didn't understand. I proceeded to tell him how he *always* (he loves absolute statements, by the way) did something and *never* did some other thing. I'm sure you get the gist of the situation.

This fight happened between working around the house and leaving to go somewhere, so during a lull he stormed off to take a shower . . . wearing nothing but a towel. When he got to the bathroom, he made sure to slam the door hard enough for me to hear his frustration. I was indignant, so I rushed back and yelled something sassy and colorful at him from outside the door. His response? He grunted something I couldn't hear, struck his strongest kung fu stance (cue towel dropping to the floor), pulled back his fist, and full-on ninja punched clear through our bathroom door (which was *not* on the list of projects for our little house). A second later I peered curiously through our new door hole, only to see my husband standing there with a stunned look on his face, posing like a ninja in his birthday suit.

Surprised and overwhelmed at the ridiculousness of the moment, we both started laughing uncontrollably! Argument over. (By the way, in case you're concerned about Ryan's anger, don't be. He once ran over a squirrel and didn't get over it for the entire day. I'm the Hulk in our house, hands down.)

I can confidently say that God has sanctified us both a lot since that day, and by his grace he continues to do so. We are not perfect, and hopefully this story illustrates our weaknesses. Even more than that, I hope it highlights God's faithfulness.

We've come a long way in our communication. And even though we still have ninja moments, they are fewer and farther between. God has helped us establish ground rules that help us communicate in healthier ways, even when tensions rise.

For example, we've agreed to never give up during hard conversations; we keep talking. We've also learned not to let conflict stew for too long: get everything out in the open, deal with issues, and be reconciled. We've also decided to work on avoiding language, ideas, and tones used with the sole intent of hurting each other. I'm not saying we follow each rule perfectly, but we at least have a mutual understanding of what's fair.

The Bible talks about communication quite a bit. God calls us to speak wisely and with love, and to let "no corrupting talk come out of your mouth," as today's Scripture says. As believers, we're called to use speech "such as is good for building up . . . that it may give grace to those who hear." While God's Word doesn't deal with every possible argument you will face in marriage, it does deal with your heart. Jesus knows that if he has our hearts, he'll have our tongues. Additionally, Jesus gives us the power and counsel of the Holy Spirit to help us act with wisdom, even in the middle of a heated argument.

Arguments and anger are like fires: you have to purposely put them out or they'll torch everything. As wives, we can pursue our husbands by diffusing heated situations *and* not throwing more wood on the fire. We're not perfect, but we've found that the following three categories for communication (what we say and how we say it) help us discern what's healthy and what's not.

Off-Limits Communication: Some words will never help your marriage. Examples: name calling, insults, demeaning or abusive language and tones, and expressing ideas aimed solely at destroying your marriage. Threatening divorce and using phrases like "I should have married so-and-so," or "I knew marrying you was a mistake," are never good. Specifically defining "off-limits" words, phrases, and ideas creates agreement about what's fair long before an argument erupts.

Unhelpful and Unproductive Communication: Words should always be intentional and "good for building up" (Ephesians 4:29). Unhelpful and unproductive talk isn't necessarily mean, but it doesn't build up or kindle love between you and your husband. One big example for us is the flippant use of absolutes like "You always" and "You never." Those phrases paint with broad, often inaccurate brush strokes. Dismissive language also falls into this category. Mumbling "Whatever" under your breath before leaving the room is passive, dismissive, unhelpful, and immature. It does nothing to move you toward reconciliation, which is God's mandate for healthy conflict resolution. Creating a ground rule for communication that makes you aware of unhelpful communication habits will help you both speak more intentionally.

Wise Communication: Finally, wisdom compels us to act in ways that are life giving and marriage preserving. Many arguments between Ryan and me could have been used to actually build our relationship if only we would have had them at a wise time and in the right location. How many big fights happen late at night because you're both tired and impatient? That's probably not the best time to dig up deep frustration about sensitive issues like sex, money, or unresolved conflict. Exercise wisdom in when and where you engage in difficult conversations; doing so kills destructive communication long before it materializes.

Fierce wives, let's pursue our husbands by lovingly diffusing harmful communication. Do so by creating ground rules for how you'll talk to each other, sticking to them, listening, and asking God to give you wisdom in where and when you discuss difficult issues. Words are powerful; especially in marriage. And as a wife, no one's words hold more power in your husband's life than yours. Speak wisely; choose words, tones, and timing that will give life.

REFLECT

What ground rules (spoken or unspoken) do you have for communication in your marriage? Are there "no fly" zones?

How can you exercise greater wisdom in your communication? Give at least one example where you could have improved.

PRAY

Ask the Holy Spirit for discernment in how you speak to each other and for your motivations to be clear and loving.

Pursuit 27

ACT

Write out a set of proposed ground rules for communication in your household. Start with the three categories we covered today and fill each one in appropriately. Be as thorough as possible.

When you're finished, sit down with your husband, discuss what you wrote, and reach a mutual understanding. Then, sign the paper together and pray for agreement as you live it out.

(If your husband is going through his own 31-Day Pursuit Challenge, he'll be reading the same thing. Definitely craft your ground rules together.)

____ *Check here when you've completed this pursuit.*

FIELD NOTES

Thoughts, feelings, or observations about today's pursuit?

To love someone
means to see him as
God intended him.

FYODOR DOSTOEVSKY

DAY
28

Faith-Fueled Feelings

But the fruit of the Spirit is love, joy, peace, patience, kindness,
goodness, faithfulness, gentleness, self-control; against such things
there is no law. And those who belong to Christ Jesus have
crucified the flesh with its passions and desires.

GALATIANS 5:22–24

Recently on a drive home from a fun evening out with the kiddos
and our friends, Ryan and I got into it. I began rehashing one of
that evening's earlier conversations where I felt like he was a jerk
to me in front of our friends. I was especially frustrated because
even though he thought he was helping, his words were having
the opposite effect.

A few minutes in, he interrupted me, "Lately it seems like your
default response to things, situations, or relationships that you
don't like or feel uncomfortable with, is anger. Did you know
there are other ways you can respond?" I just sat there quietly,

steaming with anger and growing more defensive. But deep down I knew he was right. I hated to admit it (and didn't until many moments later), but he was absolutely right.

Frustration and anger are not good defaults; I'm speaking from experience. For years, I'd get angry as my first response to situations that I didn't like. But there are (many) other, more productive, more uplifting responses I can choose from. I can still deal with how I feel without letting it turn to anger.

God has taught me that my anger isn't the product of what happens to me or around me; it's a result of what's going on in my heart (Proverbs 4:23) in areas that haven't been fully surrendered to Jesus. My out-of-control emotional responses begin when I let how I feel—my passions and desires—rule my heart instead of trusting in the truth that Jesus is King.

Here's what I mean: my distraught feelings come from deep insecurity. I get riled up if I think I've failed, disappointed someone (especially my husband), or am a victim of injustice. My anger is my defense mechanism, but it's always activated by underlying feelings of insecurity—that if I don't stand up for myself and my interests, no one will. But that's just not true.

Because of the message of the gospel—that I am forever loved, accepted, and defended by Christ—I can simply rest. I don't need to be in control, I'm not my last line of defense, and it's fine if things feel unfair at times. Bear in mind that I'm not saying the gospel is good because it permits and enables wives to be passive or spineless—it doesn't. The gospel is good because it frees us from being slaves to our emotions. The gospel is good because in it, I don't have to have the last word. And finally, the gospel is good because it's the never-changing truth that Christ reigns and his victory is secure.

Fierce wife, let's pursue our husbands by surrendering our unhealthy emotional responses to Jesus. Understand that you will never be perfect (Romans 3:23), but still, nothing will quench Christ's great love for you (Romans 5:8). Trust that the Holy Spirit is at work in your life, redeeming you, restoring you, and producing life-giving fruit in you.

Today's Bible passage is one of my favorites. Paul is reminding the church in Galatia what it looks like to be fully surrendered to Christ and led by the Spirit. He says that "those who belong to Christ have crucified the flesh with its passions and desires" (Galatians 5:24). The type of passion he's talking about is unhinged impulse—where emotions are running things. Isn't that exactly what we're talking about? But Paul shows us a better way, a Spirit-driven way that includes love, joy, peace, patience, kindness, goodness, faithfulness, gentleness, and self-control. Sounds great, but here's the tricky part: you can't manufacture fruit. *You must bear it.* It's tempting to say, "From now on, I'll try harder to have more self-control." That's not how the gospel works. That's legalism, and it leads to death.

What Paul is describing is the fruit of someone who has been crucified in their flesh, with Christ (Galatians 2:20), and is radically changed as a result. His goodness wells up in them and overflows into their lives as tangible fruit of the Spirit.

So what can you do? When emotions run high, run to Christ.

Ask for help—not just to behave better, but to believe more. Then trust that God's Word is true, that you are loved, and that you can rest in him no matter how tumultuous things feel. Trust in God's grace more than your feelings at the moment. Emotions and feelings will fade, but his love for you will never fade.

REFLECT

How do you typically handle emotions?

How can you trust in your identity in Christ more in times when your emotions would lead you elsewhere?

PRAY

Ask the Holy Spirit to be with you when you feel. Ask God to build your faith and allow it to bear fruit in your life.

Pursuit 28

ACT

⏱ ⏱ ◔ | $ $ $

Do these exercises and carve out thirty minutes to talk them over with your husband. Be vulnerable with God and with your husband, pursuing your man through vulnerability.

1.) Read Galatians 5.

a.) Two areas where I get angry/frustrated in my marriage are:

b.) The fruit produced in me by the Holy Spirit is:

c.) How does this fruit liberate me from these feelings of anger?

2.) Read John 15:1–17.

   a.) Two ways I can "abide" in Jesus more in my marriage are:

3.) Read John 16. Spend fifteen minutes in prayer, inviting the Holy Spirit to help you (a) bear fruit, (b) abide in him, and (c) pursue your husband in love and truth.

After you pray, spend a few minutes writing down what God shared with you, and review it with your husband.

___ *Check here when you've completed this pursuit.*

FIELD NOTES

Thoughts, feelings, or observations about today's pursuit?

DAY

29

Fifteen Seconds a Day

Let him kiss me with the kisses of his mouth!
For your love is better than wine.

SONG OF SOLOMON 1:2

The entire book of Song of Solomon opens with a bride confessing her love. As today's verse shows, she launched her pursuit by beckoning for a kiss: "Let him kiss me with the kisses of his mouth!" Kissing almost always marks the beginning of intense romantic physical affection. That's certainly the case for this couple. It's a part of their mutual pursuit from the outset, and it's a part of their exchange the entire book through. Don't you find it remarkable how something *so* ancient is still *so* good? Kissing is intimate, kissing is fun, and kissing is powerful. As it turns out, kissing is even more powerful than we thought.

Ryan and I met a couple at church who had been married for more than thirty years. They had faced many valleys and trials in their marriage (cancer was one of them), yet they were clearly best friends and possessed intense joy. As we were chatting with Tim, the husband, Ryan asked him point-blank, "How have you stuck together for so long?" I held my breath at the bold question; we had just met these people, and my husband can be a little intense.

Tim confidently replied without hesitation, "The fifteen-second kiss." Intrigued, Ryan inquired more and Tim explained, "Every day, my wife and I give each other a fifteen-second kiss. It's long enough that you can't fake it. It forces us to connect."

Neither Ryan nor I had ever heard of purposefully timing a kiss, and of course he asked me if I thought we should try it (he was more than excited to give it a shot). "Of course!" I said. We had to try it.

Ryan and I kiss often enough, or so I thought. But Tim helped us realize that we don't usually kiss for more than a few seconds. Most of the time our longer kisses are reserved for the bedroom; every other time they're pretty "pecky." I'm not sure why our kisses have gotten shorter; we never seemed to have a problem with inappropriately long kissing when we were dating. So, we gave it a shot, and after a few days of fifteen-second kisses, we discovered a few things.

First, fifteen seconds isn't that long . . . except when you're timing a kiss. It's like time slows down. We burn through fifteen seconds all the time without thinking about it. Kissing on a timer feels unnaturally lengthy, but that didn't last long. In our first few attempts at the fifteen-second kiss, we were both awkwardly aware of the time because it was new. It felt forced, clunky, and silly, but it didn't take long for us to get lost. We often let life get too busy to allow ourselves to "get lost" in anything, let alone an act of romance. Kissing for fifteen seconds was a refreshing reminder that we can truly get lost in our affection for one another.

The second thing we learned is that you can't easily kiss for an extended period of time and not feel closer to one another. Kissing is intimate. We found that as we got lost in kissing, we were going *somewhere* together, but neither of us knew where. The thing about getting lost with someone is that it actually helps you *find* them. We were also reminded how much the act of kissing makes us feel closer, which is huge for me. I can tell when Ryan and I aren't close or on the same page during the day, and my level of angst seems to compound over time. Kissing for fifteen seconds reunites us and helps us both feel close. Kissing refocuses us on *who* we are to each other. When you're "kissably close" to your husband, it helps you remember who he is as a person. It's easy to start seeing your husband as a roommate, but kissing him will remind you of his distinctly human qualities (good and bad) that you fell in love with in the first place.

Finally, kissing tends to lead to intimacy and sex. Have you ever refused dessert because it didn't sound good, only to try a small bite and ask for an entire helping? Kissing has a similar effect. You may not be in the mood for sex or physical closeness when you start the kiss, but there's a reasonably good chance your mind will change. . . and in marriage, that's a good thing!

REFLECT

Think back on your best kiss ever with your spouse. What made it so special?

What role does kissing play in your daily lives? Why do you usually kiss, who initiates, and when do kisses usually happen?

PRAY

Ask God to remove any barriers or uneasiness as you work on your physical connection. Pray for willingness and opportunities to make kissing a priority.

Pursuit 29

ACT

🕐 ◔ ◔ | $ $ $

Brush those teeth! It's time for a fifteen-second kiss. Make sure your husband is ready for today's pursuit as well, so you're both on the same page. Chat about your thoughts on the fifteen-second kiss idea, then go for it! Do your best to kiss without motive or agenda, but don't be surprised if it leads elsewhere. Consider making the fifteen-second kiss a daily part of your lives.

(If your husband is going through his own 31-Day Pursuit Challenge, he'll be reading the same thing! Go ahead and surprise him by keeping it going longer than expected.)

___ *Check here when you've completed this pursuit.*

FIELD NOTES

Thoughts, feelings, or observations about today's pursuit?

HEADS-UP!

Day 31 is almost here! Ready?

DAY
30

Designed and Assigned

Then the LORD God said, "It is not good that the man should be alone; I will make him a helper fit for him."

GENESIS 2:18

God's Word calls husbands heads of their families as Christ is the head of the church (Ephesians 5:23). Along with that assignment, they're charged with loving, serving, and leading their wives, just as Christ loves, serves, and leads his bride, the church (Ephesians 5:25–33). You may be familiar with that language, but let's pause and think about what it means for a second . . . If our husbands are entrusted with loving us wives how Christ loved his bride, then they're called to serve sacrificially, selflessly, tenderly, and so much more. That's a tall order! They are called to the same standard of love displayed by God's only Son while he lived on earth and died to rescue humanity. It's a tough gig, to say the least, but they have help—that's where we come in.

Will your husband perfectly fulfill his role 100 percent of the time? Nope. Is he aware of his imperfection and in need of help, encouragement, and support as he grows? Probably. The good news is that God is alive and working in your husband's life daily. And as wives we must remember that many times the way God chooses to help our husbands is through us. As today's verse shows us, that's been God's design since the garden of Eden: "I will make him a helper fit for him."

We get front-row seats to exactly what is happening in our husbands' lives and hearts. Not only are we in a good position to see our husbands up close, but we're in the right posture: emotionally attuned and naturally inclined to help. God custom made us women with an innate ability to sense what's going on beneath the surface, then he placed us in the closest possible proximity to our husbands—by their sides—to help them.

It's a beautiful moment when you can be an instrument of God's grace in action as he sanctifies and strengthens your husband. Sometimes those moments are simple and profound, requiring little effort. Other times, you must engage in spiritual warfare through prayer, reading God's Word, asking intentional questions, and patiently listening or observing.

Today's pursuit is about using intentional, specific words of encouragement to help your husband become the man he is called to be. Consider the following five phrases and how they can tangibly help your husband. Each one has helped me encourage Ryan in daily life, but also whenever he feels vulnerable and weak:

1: *"I trust you."* Do you trust your husband to lead you well? Do you trust God to use your husband for your good and his glory? If so, tell him! Take time to look him in the eye and let him know. If you're in the middle of rebuilding trust with your husband, pick out a few specific areas or reasons why you trust him *now,* and explain why that's the case. Either way, be specific; it will enhance the encouragement.

2: *"I believe in you."* I asked Ryan how it makes him feel when I tell him this, and he said, "Anyone else in the world can tell me they believe in me, but it's a thousand times more powerful when I hear it from you." You know your husband more than anyone else (good, bad, ugly), and if anyone can be accurately critical, it's you. There's nothing like the consistent, genuine belief spouses place in each other. That kind of belief says, "God is working in you. He isn't done with you, and neither am I."

3: *"I'm with you."* Your husband longs for your partnership and complicity. Remind him you're both on the same side and you're glad to be spending your life with him. Remind him that there's nothing you can't get through together, and that God brought you together for his divine purposes. Those words will be an adrenaline shot directly to his heart—filling him with energy, faith, life, and boldness.

4: *"I desire you."* We ladies get a ton of press for wanting to be desired and pursued. While men are definitely different, most men want to be desired as well. And yes, I do mean physically. Your man wants to make you swoon, he wants to be strong for you, and he wants you to desire him because he's enough for you—and more. Let him sweep you off your feet, remain swoonable, and make sure he knows you desire him on every level. If this is a struggle, remind yourself of who he is to you and why you were attracted to him in the first place. Let yourself indulge in wanting him. He is your man, your love, your best friend, and your life partner.

5: *"I know you're not perfect, but I love you anyway."* This one's the most important. When you recognize your husband's faults and still love him (and vice versa), that's grace. When you express your love for him in the midst of his most obvious flaws, it's an opportunity for him to see the love of Christ in one of the most vivid ways possible. This is the kind of love that pushes us closer to Jesus, and it's the kind of love that we're all called to display in marriage. When Ryan hears this phrase—"I know you're not perfect, but I still love you"—it disarms his defenses, allows him to be vulnerable, and builds him up in entirely unique ways.

Fierce wife, you have an unmatched opportunity to be a force for encouragement and help for your husband. Nobody knows him like you, and trust me when I say this: your husband is looking to *you* for help every single day. He is a gift and blessing to you, just as you are a gift and a blessing to him. You've been custom designed and assigned; you can do this! Never underestimate the power you have to help and encourage your husband.

REFLECT

Have you been encouraging your husband lately? If so, how has that helped him? If not, why not?

PRAY

Ask God for insight on how to encourage your husband. Pray for help seeing your husband as God sees him and for help seeing yourself as God sees you.

Pursuit 30

ACT

🕐 🕑 🕑 | $ $ $

I'm sure you can already see where this is going. Today, pick one or two of the phrases above to encourage your husband. Observe him, ask him questions to find out how he's feeling, pray, and be specific about each encouragement. Extend grace, show him love, and pursue his heart, trusting God to open it to receive.

____ *Check here when you've completed this pursuit.*

FIELD NOTES

Thoughts, feelings, or observations about today's pursuit?

HEADS-UP!

Tomorrow is the big day. Are you feeling ready?

There is no more lovely, friendly and charming relationship, communion, or company than a good marriage.

MARTIN LUTHER

DAY

31

Celebrating a Life of Pursuit

I do not account my life of any value nor as precious to myself, if only I may finish my course and the ministry that I received from the Lord Jesus, to testify to the gospel of the grace of God.

ACTS 20:24

Congratulations, my fierce friend! You've made it! While this is the end of our journey together, today marks the beginning of the rest of your life pursuing your husband. Before we started, I called this book a crutch, which you might have found strange. I hope my wording makes more sense now. If you recall, we read this quote from C. S. Lewis:

Duty is only a substitute for love (of God and of other people) like a crutch which is a substitute for a leg. Most of us need the crutch at times; but of course it is idiotic to use the crutch when our own legs (our own loves, tastes,

habits etc.) can do the journey on their own. They are
helpful and necessary for a time, but eventually you need
to walk without them.[2]

It's time to drop the crutches, walk without them, and forge onward as a woman in lifelong pursuit. Loving your husband out of duty is fine and sometimes necessary, but it's not the ideal. Maybe you started this book out of duty, or maybe duty is where you are today. Or, maybe you never had crutches and this book fueled your already present desire. Wherever you're at, keep going!

The more enjoyable route—the way you were made to operate—is to pursue your husband out of love for him that is fueled by how deeply and eternally you are loved in Christ. Hopefully every day of this challenge has brought you closer to that end.

I approached this book with two objectives in mind. (Ryan and I approached our respective halves of the 31-Day Pursuit Challenge with the same objectives.) First, I wanted to show you the depth of Christ's love and pursuit of you and then illustrate how experiencing it fuels the way you pursue your husband.

Second, I aimed to help you think differently about what it means to pursue your husband. My hope and prayer is that this book has helped you to grow in skill, creativity, and conviction in the ways and consistency with which you pursue the man God has given you.

Today's verse has become an essential part of daily life for Ryan and me. It's posted intentionally around our house to remind us of where our identity, worth, and purpose is and should be found: in Christ. This life isn't about me—it's about Jesus. It's a reminder that my days are fleeting and my treasure is in heaven, and that this life isn't valuable in itself, but only as a gift from God for his ultimate glory. It's my daily encouragement to "finish my course and the ministry that I received from the Lord Jesus, to testify to the gospel of the grace of God," and to love *my* husband the specific way God has called *me*.

As I mentioned, today marks a new beginning for you in fulfilling a portion of God's call on your life. From here forward, you can forge on with a fresh understanding of how to pursue your husband in light of Jesus' pursuit of you. Now's the time for you to put your new knowledge to work. It's time to drop the crutches and walk in love, with boldness and conviction.

At this point, the two biggest challenges to your pursuit are time and creativity. Will you be actively pursuing your husband one year from now? How about ten? Twenty? Will your pursuit actively change and evolve as your husband changes? By God's grace, you—we—can answer yes to each of those questions, but it will require intentionality.

That's your final challenge: to pursue your husband joyfully, confidently, and intentionally for the rest of your life. Rest assured that Jesus will help you every step of the way; simply fix your eyes on him, remember how relentlessly God has pursued you in Christ, and let his love fuel your pursuit of your husband every moment until the day you die.

REFLECT

Which pursuit challenge has had the most impact on you? On your husband? Why?

MY PRAYER FOR YOU

God, thank you for pursuing us in such radical ways. I pray that this fierce wife would deeply and clearly understand that she is your beloved—and that you sacrificed your only Son in pursuit of her soul as well as her husband's. Only out of that knowledge and understanding can she first experience you in a real way, and second, live and pursue her husband out of your love for her. May any fear or timidity in pursuing her husband be driven out by your perfect love. Anchor her in you and lead her to be selfless and generous in her pursuit of her husband's heart. Holy Spirit, I ask that you break down any walls that would divide and separate this wife from her husband. Thank you for always pursuing her, God. Lead her to do the same with her husband every day—for as long as they both shall live. In Jesus' name I ask and believe. Amen.

Pursuit 31

ACT

⏱⏱⏱ | $ $ $

Commemorate the start of your lifelong pursuit. Celebrate! Do something ridiculous, extravagant, off-script, and off-the-charts unconventional. Now is your opportunity to pull out all the stops.

Hopefully you've taken some time to think about and plan for today (observing the "Heads-Up!" notifications along the way). If not, no worries! Do something radically spontaneous—your husband is sure to love whatever you come up with.

(If your husband is going through his 31-Day Pursuit Challenge on the same schedule, you'll be doing this together. Feel free to plan this one with him in the name of mutual pursuit.)

___ Check here when you've completed this pursuit. Great work.

FINAL PURSUIT CHALLENGE

Pursue your husband for the rest of your life by starting with a custom Pursuit Plan. See the following pages for details and help with this challenge.

God will look to every soul
like its first love because
He is its first love.

C. S. LEWIS

A Lifelong Pursuit Challenge

Over the past thirty-one days, we've explored how to love our husbands with selflessness, service, affection, friendship, and thoughtfulness—all in light of the gospel. How can you make each avenue of pursuit a daily part of your life? What does your lifelong pursuit of your husband look like from this day forward? What habits will you adopt daily, weekly, monthly, and yearly?

Complete the Pursuit Plan template on the following page. Feel free to share it with your husband if you feel led. Then, purpose to follow it until you've learned to pursue your husband out of habit. Set reminders on your calendar, and most importantly, follow through. Revisit your plan regularly to keep it up to date and fresh in your mind. Consider journaling about your pursuit as a way of tracking personal and marital growth.

Time will pass and life will happen regardless of how intentionally you pursue your husband. If you commit to habit the actions of pursuit, the time and life that you share with your husband will be that much richer. Fierce wife, pursue your husband out of joy! Have fun following him for the rest of your life. Laugh, talk, touch, dream, be intimate, and spend still, quiet moments beside him with pure freedom of joy. You are radically pursued by Jesus, now go and radically pursue the one he's placed in your life . . . for the rest of your life.

My Pursuit Plan

NAME _____ DATE _____

HUSBAND'S NAME _____

Over the course of this 31-Day Pursuit Challenge, I've learned to pursue my husband as Christ pursues me by:

Given what I've learned, I will pursue my husband consistently through the following intentional actions of love:

Daily	Weekly	Monthly	Yearly

Today marks the beginning of the rest of my life pursuing my husband. I understand that I am called to love him and that doing so is my privilege as his wife. I cannot do it alone, but it won't happen without my effort. By God's grace, I will love my husband well until the day I die, and not a moment less.

SIGNED _____

50 Creative Date Ideas

You know your area, your passions, and your husband better than anyone, so naturally you'd plan the best dates for him. Here are some ideas we came up with just in case you feel stuck. This list is far from ultimate, but it's a start!*

1. Complete one bucket list item for each of you.
2. Go stargazing and find at least three new constellations.
3. Get up early, grab coffee, and watch the sunrise.
4. Make a meal with *only* what you find at a farmer's market.
5. Pick a spot on a map and just start driving.
6. Try rock climbing. Do at least one dyno each.
7. Rent kayaks and go paddling.
8. Go to a jazz club and dance to *all* the slow tunes.
9. Visit a zoo or an aquarium.
10. Check out a new band.
11. Get theatre tickets to a local play.
12. Begin training for a 5k together.
13. Do one "guy thing" you'd never do otherwise.
14. Go fishing and cook your catch over a fire.
15. Sign up for a cooking class.
16. See a comedy show.
17. Visit a local art gallery.
18. Go paintballing. Mutiny against everyone else.
19. Go to a trampoline park (if you can find one nearby).
20. Catch a movie at a drive-in. Kiss more than usual.
21. Go on a dessert tasting tour to at least three places.

22. Take swing dancing lessons.
23. Go paddle boarding. Make a point to fall in the water.
24. Do something that gets your adrenaline pumping.
25. Take a rowboat out on a pond at sunset.
26. Go for a jog in the rain.
27. Volunteer at a local homeless shelter.
28. Try an improv class.
29. Plan a surprise weekend getaway.
30. Go to a new restaurant you'd normally never visit.
31. Sign up for a mud run.
32. Have a picnic in the park.
33. Head to an arcade for an old-school game tournament.
34. Go away for the weekend. No plans, just go.
35. Attend a local poetry reading.
36. Try a workout class neither of you has ever tried.
37. Have a bonfire on the beach. Make s'mores.
38. Visit a botanical garden.
39. Take salsa dancing lessons.
40. Go on a local used bookstore tour.
41. Do something touristy in your hometown.
42. Go to a matinee. Critique the film over lunch.
43. Take SCUBA lessons.
44. Hike a nearby trail (one you both find challenging).
45. Order takeout and play a game you both love.
46. Go ice skating. Grab cocoa nearby and people watch.
47. Visit a local landmark and have dinner nearby.
48. Ride bikes through your city and grab street tacos.
49. Get a couple's massage. Rather, give each other massages!
50. Have a night in, no phones, no distractions. Get frisky.

*All the activities on this list should be done safely and responsibly. Anything you do is at your own risk. We're not responsible for your safety! Have fun, be careful, live to tell the story.

Additional Resources

Our mission is simple: point couples to Christ. It drives everything we do. We write weekly on our blog and release new content daily via social media.

FIND US ONLINE

FierceMarriage.com
FierceMarriage.com/List
Facebook.com/FierceMarriage
Instagram.com/FierceMarriage
YouTube.com/FierceMarriage
Twitter.com/FierceMarriage

RECOMMENDED BOOKS

For a list of books we love, visit FierceMarriage.com/Resources.

SHARE THIS BOOK WITH A FRIEND

If you'd like to share this book with a friend, please direct them to 31DayPursuit.com.

DO YOU HAVE FEEDBACK OR A STORY?

If this book has helped you, please share your story with us. If we can improve or fix anything about this resource, please let us know. To do either, send an email to care@fiercemarriage.com.

WANT TO LEAVE A REVIEW?

If you've enjoyed this book, we'd be honored if you wrote an honest review wherever you purchased your copy (Amazon.com or elsewhere). In it, share how God is working in your marriage and watch as your story ministers to others. You never know who might read it and be encouraged.

GROUP STUDY LEADERS

If you would like to lead a small group based on this devotional, bulk discounts are available (8+ copies). Please email details to care@fiercemarriage.com and someone will be in touch shortly.

SPEAKING REQUESTS

For speaking inquiries, please visit FierceMarriage.com/Speaking.

Notes

1. DAY 23: UNTIRING LOVE

The quoted excerpt from Louisa May Alcott's *Little Women* can be found on page 87 of the Signet Classics edition, published in 2012. It was first published in 1868.

2. DAY 31: CELEBRATING A LIFE OF PURSUIT

The quote from C. S. Lewis beginning, "Duty is only a substitute for love (of God and of other people) like a crutch which is a substitute for a leg," is from *Letters of C. S. Lewis*, in a letter dated July 18, 1957, to Joan Lancaster. The collection is published by Harvest Books, copyrighted 1966.

And so train the young women
to love their husbands and children . . .

Titus 2:4